SIMON & SCHUSTER
CROSSWORD PUZZLE BOOK

Series 248

New challenges in the original series,
containing 50 never-before-published crosswords

Edited by JOHN M. SAMSON

A Fireside Book
Published by Simon & Schuster
New York   London   Toronto   Sydney

FIRESIDE
Rockefeller Center
1230 Avenue of the Americas
New York, NY 10020

For information about special discounts for bulk purchases,
please contact Simon & Schuster Special Sales at
1-800-456-6798 or business@simonandschuster.com

Designed by Sam Bellotto Jr.

Manufactured in the United States of America

10 9 8 7 6 5 4 3 2 1

ISBN-13: 978-0-7432-8313-7

COMPLETE ANSWERS WILL BE FOUND AT THE BACK.

FOREWORD

LAZY CLUER by Harvey Estes

(Harvey was feeling lazy, so he decided to write just half as many clues for this puzzle. There is one clue for each row and column. In each of them, the clues for both of the answers in that row or column have been placed side by side. Which comes first and where one ends and the other begins is for you to decide.)

ACROSS

1 Evening of the French horn player
11 Like a button richly decorated
12 Texas players' beginning of all-time low
13 Monty Hall offering Mexican food item
15 Rockers' chance to work old pump handle
16 In children's lit he hides girl crying "Uncle!"
17 Run film projector part
18 Newsman Peter drinks like a boxer
19 Steal part from a car
20 Still new coin
21 Most recent site for British magazine

DOWN

1 Scoundrel goes after Moby Dick
2 Talk over estimator's phrase
3 Aware of woman in a Poe work
4 Darkened collar
5 Classify WW2 arena
6 Merman takes five
7 Sure confidence game
8 Period of dark marks on the face
9 Give the okay to slanted writing
10 Notice bridge mistake
14 Terrific school in the ACC

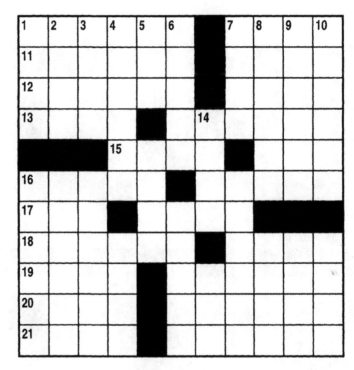

The Margaret Award winner is Manny Nosowsky's TRIPOD TRILOGY.

JOHN M. SAMSON

IF YOU ENJOY OUR PUZZLES, HERE'S MORE TO EXPLORE.

Simon & Schuster has been publishing outstanding crossword puzzle books every year since 1924—a grand tradition that continues into the twenty-first century.

The world's first and longest-running crossword series continues its tradition of all brand-new and totally original puzzles, constructed by top experts in the field. Editor John M. Samson promises another year of prime cruciverbal wizardry that will keep your brow furrowed and your mind spinning.

So get out your pens or pencils, sharpen your wits, and get ready for months of brain-teasing fun!

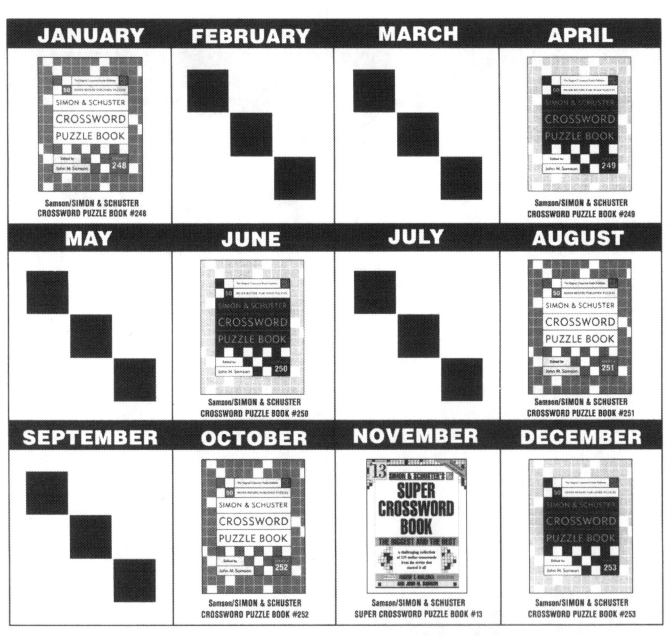

1 GEOMETRICKS   by Jay Sullivan
Solve this one with a compass pencil.

ACROSS

1 Jeer
6 Missing link
12 Greek I
16 Chair person
17 Skater Surya
18 Big belt
19 Cool coterie?
21 Tropical torch
22 Networking equipment
23 Rite answer
24 Trite
25 Blessed event?
26 It's just not right?
28 Word on the street about you
29 TV band
30 Short retriever
31 Notre Dame has one
34 Take a few courses
36 It's hot
38 City of the Roman Empire
42 Exploits
44 "Absolutely!"
46 Name names
48 Leftover
49 Pawn stop?
52 Poor reception
53 "St. Elmo's Fire" star
55 Long-running NBC show
56 NHL infraction
58 "A Day Without Rain" singer
59 Tee off
61 Not up to snuff
63 Action figures?
64 Sixth-day creation
66 Ballpark fig.
68 Fashion monogram
70 "We're downsizing . . ." is one?
74 A Gandhi
78 Upright
79 ___-de-France
80 Maroons
81 Gone fishing, perhaps
82 eBay, e.g.?
84 It's a sin
85 Impassive
86 Mime Muse
87 "Jolly Roger" pirate
88 Museum pieces
89 Napoleon III's "Waterloo"

DOWN

1 Marks for life
2 "An American in Paris" star
3 In timely fashion
4 In irons
5 Ulster cloth
6 Basic skills
7 Luau treat
8 Add vitamins
9 Macbeth's nemesis
10 Apportion
11 Will of "Murder, She Wrote"
12 Constantinople, now
13 In arrears
14 Mayan ruins site
15 Quick on one's feet
20 Fancy flapjack
24 Bighorn's bleat
26 There are lots of them
27 Senior citizen
31 Love to pieces
32 Argentine president (1974–76)
33 Stored up
35 Totalizer
37 In any way, shape, or form
39 Fanatic
40 Light-headed?
41 Toils (away)
43 Hit sign
45 Binet's concern
47 Hula hoop?
50 Southfork family
51 Team up
54 Bond in layers
57 Fever blister
60 Lake Wobegon's favorite son
62 It's not to be believed
65 "Go on . . ."
67 Angling leaders
69 Takes potshots
70 Young colts
71 "To recap . . ."
72 Candy man
73 Remain stationary, at sea
75 Troy story
76 Oscar de la ___
77 ___ Martin
80 Reception participants
82 Former boomer
83 Six, in binary

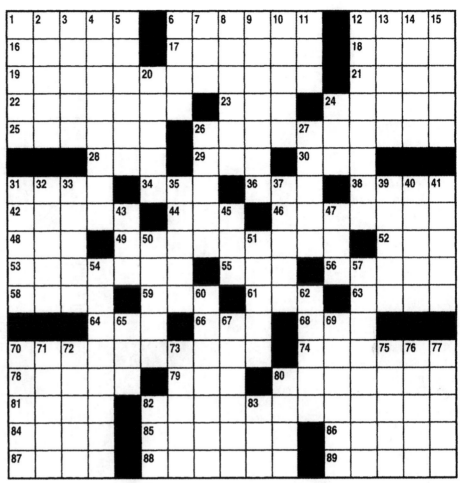

WRITE-IN CANDIDATES by Ray Hamel
The Socialist Party candidate at 20 Across ran unsuccessfully again in 1905.

ACROSS

1 Candelabra crystals
7 Playful mammal
12 Suvari in "American Beauty"
16 Scottish goblin
17 Southern lady
18 Garden snake locale?
19 Legendary Chicago Fire figure
20 He ran for mayor of Oakland (1901)
22 James Monroe's portraitist
23 Delt neighbor
24 Galápagos lizard
25 He ran for Congress in Pennsylvania (1962)
29 Historical spans
30 Edge a doily
31 Kowtowing
36 Spike TV, formerly
37 Org. with a panda logo
38 Busy home
39 Amana product
40 Have room
41 Knockoff
42 Icy precip
43 He was elected to Parliament (1969)
46 Cut closely
48 Cheers for the toreador
49 Boston nine, for short
50 To a degree
51 11th U.S. President
52 ___ out of (withdraw from)
53 An ID
56 Big beef cut
58 Clean Air Act enforcement gp.
59 Boyfriend
60 He ran for governor of Calif. (1934)
63 Judicial inquiry
67 Pricey pitcher?
68 Choir repertoire
69 He was elected to Parliament (1848)
72 Dress size
73 Running birds
74 Diner patron
75 Composer of ten symphonies
76 Singer Coolidge
77 Resided
78 Alka-Seltzer boy of the 1950s

DOWN

1 Lockheed L-188 Electra, e.g.
2 Memorize anew
3 Thoughtful one?
4 They may be tipped
5 Zebrula mothers
6 Spook
7 Verb used by Perry Mason
8 Coach
9 "Trading Spaces" ntwk.
10 Hartford Insurance logo
11 Take over for 67 Across
12 Place for dishes?
13 Old Norse epic
14 One of the noble gases
15 "___ of the Five Towns": Bennett
21 Fairy-tale meanie
23 "Milord" singer Edith
26 Datebook headings
27 Alexander and Eleniak
28 Haughty refusal
32 Expensive watch
33 "She's All I ___ Had": Ricky Martin
34 Name-before-marriage
35 Effective razer
37 Ring wearer
38 Salma in "Frida"
40 Flu symptom
41 Landed on
42 Kaput
43 Doorframe part
44 Leghorn's resting site
45 Congressional channel
46 Belarus, prev.
47 ___ polloi
51 Like an AKC dog
52 Ronny Howard role
53 Nautical distance
54 Canonized
55 Shrubbery seller
57 Liqueur for Zorba
58 Deb's date
59 Bill Clinton's birthname
61 Garbo's "The Mysterious Lady" leading man
62 Chintzy
63 Anagram verb of RAVE
64 Ventura County "Valley"
65 Rabbit tail
66 "___ Most Unusual Day"
70 Left, in the field
71 Shoshonean tribe
72 UK heads

3 CHEEP LAUGH by Bud Gillis
That's not a misspelling in the title.

ACROSS

1 Shirt-tag abbr.
4 Close a leather jacket
7 Cedar home?
11 Kremlin kingpin of yore
15 Felling tool
16 Geological span
17 Sunlight, to skin
18 Cool shade
19 **Steven Wright quip: Part 1**
22 Beyond help
23 Leonine griffin feature
24 Distinctive atmosphere
25 Act like
27 Secret motive
29 Giant of Cooperstown (with 79-A)
30 Copier cartridge
31 "Sort of" suffix
32 Yeats contemporary
34 **Quip: Part 2**
37 "Go!" preceder
38 Beetle Bailey's bed
39 Unconscious quirks
40 "Selena" star, to fans
41 Without restrictions
43 Its state fish is the cutthroat trout
45 **Quip: Part 3**
49 Bounded
50 Kind of game hen
51 Drop a pop-up, say
52 ___-TASS
54 Allowing liquor sales
55 Cookie container
58 **Quip: Part 4**
61 "You ___ saying?"
62 Latin 101 word
63 Excel
64 Waxman in "Hollywood Ending"
65 "Georgia on My Mind" trees
67 ALMA awardees
69 Seal hunter
71 Early tennis champ Lacoste
72 Stink bomb output
73 **End of quip**
76 Starr of Super Bowl I
77 Top-flight
78 Bath or place follower
79 See 29 Across
80 Award named for a TV camera tube
81 Strong desires
82 Moundsman's stat
83 Threader's target

DOWN

1 Curaçao cocktails
2 Vast area
3 Please highly
4 Buddhism branch
5 Scarcely detectable amount
6 Tire type
7 Like Urkel's voice
8 Vanity
9 Arabic's language group
10 Temblors
11 Preferences
12 Dick Tracy facial feature
13 "Go tell ___ Rhody . . ."
14 Sand trap smoother
20 Without exception
21 Brought up, as well water
26 Dem. or Rep. colleague
28 Accompany
33 Office phone button
34 Mosquito, at times
35 K–12
36 "Inka Dinka ___": Durante song
39 Sea north of Australia
41 Autumn breeze trait
42 Showy parrot
43 Marching on the beat
44 "My bad!"
45 Inflatable bed
46 Tour small towns
47 Like Sheridan Whiteside
48 A gangplank rests on it
49 Took charge of
52 Not by any means
53 Tallchief's footwear
55 Mystery woman
56 Room service, e.g.
57 Floral cake decoration
59 Nolan Ryan's Angel number
60 Reunion attendees
61 Toadish feature
64 They're cast and counted
66 Blood-boiling emotion
67 Spot for a stud
68 Enoch's grandfather
70 From a distance
74 Fay's "King Kong" role
75 Fraternity letter

4 CALL ME GOJIRA   by Sam Bellotto Jr.
Gojira (Godzilla) means "gorilla whale" in Japanese.

ACROSS

1 Restaurant alfresco
5 Knife: Slang
9 Japanese for "monster"
14 Europe-Asia border
16 Diamond corners?
18 Promotion specialists
19 Momoko Kochi portrayed her in "Godzilla"
21 Clientele
22 Porgy
23 Dr. Serizawa, to 19 Across
25 Finger-lickin' luau food
26 Place for antifreeze
28 Sans rocks
32 They're unique
34 He directed "Godzilla"
36 Cantina coin
37 CIA employee
38 Darkman's garment
39 Lass
40 Indulged
43 Keepsake
45 Dr. Serizawa's Godzilla slayer
50 Bawdy
51 Maori miss
52 Merkel in "Saratoga"
53 Earth goddess
57 Wetland
58 Two-year-old doe
62 1954 "Godzilla" star
65 Hawaiian singer
66 Canadian gas name
67 Gladstone's archrival
69 Cumshaw
70 "Once a Thief" novelist
72 Cucumber's cousin
74 Word form for "straight"
77 2004 was Godzilla's 50th
80 Takarada in "Godzilla"
81 Children's author R.L.
82 Jerks make them
83 Friend and foe of Godzilla
84 Biblical verb
85 Satirist Mort

DOWN

1 Eight-ball stick
2 Radius, e.g.
3 Twins who accompany 63 Down
4 Sommer in "The Prize"
5 Entrepreneur's org.
6 Clumsy
7 Contemporary of Micah
8 Like a hunter-gatherer
9 Hudson in "The Four Feathers"
10 Gland prefix
11 "___ Man": Yardbirds
12 Hillbilly Clampett
13 Third of trois
15 Flies like an eagle
17 Spanish wife
20 Singer Sumac
24 Jockey's whip
25 Coach Warner
27 "Eat up!"
29 Penn State coach before Paterno
30 Firefighter Red
31 Barbershop powder
33 Mrs. Fred Astaire
35 Grallatorial bird
37 "Blue Gender" director Masashi
41 Galore
42 Meadow moisture
44 Give the ___ (ogle)
45 Lady Chaplin et al.
46 Dental charges
47 Microscopy stains
48 Soothing word
49 Sen fraction
50 Unalloyed
54 "___ Love Her": Beatles
55 Minnesota city and "Ab Fab" role
56 Variety of wormwood
59 Way in to the plaza de toros
60 Three-headed foe of Godzilla
61 Pataki's party
63 Friend and foe of Godzilla
64 Muse of astronomy
65 John Galliano designs
68 Big, in a small way
71 Bookbinding leather
73 GI hangouts
74 Regatta competitor
75 H. Hughes acquistion
76 Prescription abbr.
78 Godzilla's doc?
79 Designer monogram

TRAVELING SALESPERSON*   by Nancy Salomon & Kendall Twigg
You may want to skip 48 Across until you've tried guessing the theme.

ACROSS

1 Artillery burst
6 Like some attics
11 Wren's Beau
16 Brought home takeout
17 Golfer with an army
18 Speedy
19 Issue from a dancer?*
21 Big ape
22 Roof edge
23 Biblical twin
24 Orlando arbor?
26 Have coming
28 Unable to decide
30 Pianist Dame Myra
31 Sticky attachment?*
35 Serial segment
38 Weed-killing tools
39 Musical aptitude
42 Exxon rival
43 A shutout lowers this
45 "C'mon!"
47 Bossy asset?
48 Each clue* answer, to SALESPERSON
51 Workplace watchdog gp.
52 One in a lineup
54 Keyboard key
55 Tourney type
56 Leb. neighbor
57 Two-toned predator
60 Sights for sore eyes
62 Detection system shuts down?*
65 Big name in faucets
67 "Holy moly!"
68 Tugs none too gently
72 Come clean
74 Yankee Martinez
77 Temple of the Sun worshiper
79 Violin-case item
80 Sediment of a sermonizer?*
83 Olds model
84 Put out
85 On-board board
86 Lightens up
87 Repulse
88 Pales by comparison?

DOWN

1 "Lost our lease" event
2 First-stringers
3 Hit the road
4 Deadly snake
5 Single or united
6 Physics calculation
7 Celestial bear
8 Schnauzer schnozzes
9 Pie plate
10 "Decide already!"
11 Understand, à la Heinlein
12 Singer Kitt
13 Reserve class?*
14 Steak stabbers
15 Creeps
20 Back in
25 Scholasti-cism founder
27 ___ facto
29 Sound of awe
32 Paradise lost
33 Aventis Pasteur products
34 Suffix with Peking
35 Post of etiquette
36 Frigid feelings?*
37 Gross
40 Turkish titles
41 Gad about
42 Sound boosters
44 IRS employee
46 Lawn mower brand
48 Layouts
49 Glowing review
50 Rose's Broadway beau
53 Unfathomably long time
55 Tower town
58 Refrigerator drawer
59 Egyptian cobra
61 Be a plant
63 Hotter than a pistol
64 Pull out all the stops
65 Singer Carmen
66 Alley Oop's lady
69 Nabisco's ___ Wafers
70 Work out a knot
71 Public tiff
73 Slaughter in Cooperstown
75 St. Martin, for one
76 Winter air
78 Grills
81 Guitar, slangily
82 Tanning lotion letters

6

HIGHWAY HUMOR   by Ernest Lampert
The slogan below was actually a set of signs—one set is in the Smithsonian.

ACROSS

1 ___ ex machina (artificial device)
5 Out of port
10 Insignia
16 Old Shell rival
17 W.C. Fields acknowledgment
18 Annette of "Cat People"
19 **Start of a slogan**
22 Puccini's last opera
23 End of a URL
24 Patronage
25 Watch readout, briefly
26 ___-Boy recliner
27 Tierra del Fuego tribe
28 FBI sting of the '70s
32 **More of slogan**
36 Custard apple
37 "Coffee, Tea ___?" (1973)
38 M.A. pursuer's test
39 Indigo dye
40 Stage property
41 **More of slogan**
45 Scratched
47 Mendelssohn's Third Symphony
49 "The Graduate" heroine
50 Where Dr Pepper originated
51 Inner beginning
52 Merkel in "42nd Street"
53 Axes
54 Faked out, in the NHL
55 **Source of slogan**
59 Citation aircraft company
60 Private address?
61 Suffix for Gotham
62 "___ we meet again"
63 Words before deal or boy
65 Chest muscle
66 Irrigation measure
71 **End of slogan**
74 First name in cooking
75 Stevenson's isle in Samoa
76 Miming dance
77 Pooh-pooh
78 Ratchet engagers
79 "Stupid ___ stupid does"

DOWN

1 Part of DMV
2 Genesis redhead
3 "Back in the ___": Beatles
4 Former Cub slugger
5 Two for the road
6 George Burns film
7 Short method
8 Common Mkt.
9 Southern cornbread
10 Prosper
11 Bermuda Triangle loc.
12 Take a short nap
13 Really large amount
14 Climatic scapegoat
15 Be indecisive
20 Acquired kin
21 Primordial stuff
26 Nightingale's prop
28 Lickety-split
29 Ho-hum
30 ___ yarn (confabulate)
31 It's in your bones
32 Stepped on
33 Northern hemisphere?
34 Waste allowance
35 Small sofas
37 Natural resource
40 Petitions
42 Acts like a pig
43 Minneapolis-to-Fargo hwy.
44 Harper series
46 Commune near Palermo
47 Sound upstairs
48 Office dupes, for short
50 Swell
53 Draw even with
54 Removes a typo
55 Released conditionally
56 Computer availability
57 Lineup
58 Hurries
59 High cloud
62 Antibody regulator
64 Longfellow's bell town
65 Soccer's "Black Pearl"
66 Confess
67 Alphabet run
68 "It's either them ___"
69 Jabba the Hutt's dancer
70 Start of "Jabberwocky"
72 Ceiling
73 Shrink's org.

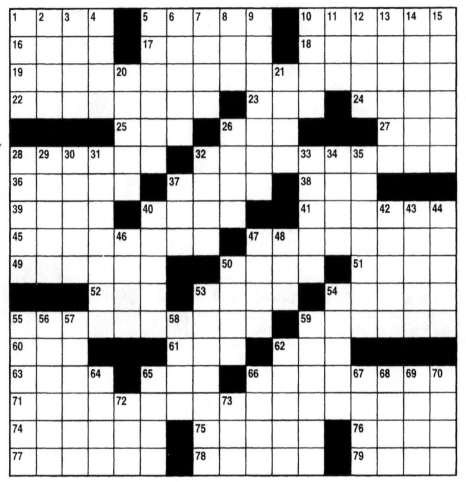

7 CHOCOHOLIC'S DELIGHT   by Patrick Jordan
SpongeBob fans should know the answer to 87 Across.

ACROSS

1 Emulate Salome
6 Yawning
11 A Baltimore clipper has two
16 Affection, in Amiens
17 Birth-related
18 Member of one's class
19 Like many celebrity bios
21 Duplicity
22 ". . . and children of all ___"
23 Intense displeasure
24 Freedom movement, briefly
26 Sitting on
27 Greeted the judge
28 Cheesy sandwich
30 Sinuous firework
32 Knight
34 "Say what?" expressions
36 Toothpaste form
37 "So that's what you're up to!"
40 Falsify data
46 Score
48 Water barrier
49 Dealer buster
50 Demonic entities
51 Turns with a spatula
53 City near Dayton
54 Clinton's attorney general
55 Helped oneself
56 Less punctual
58 Black box that cost $1 in 1900
61 Titan scores
62 Lawn layer
63 First Lady McKinley
64 Prom setting
66 Bath cloth
70 Shampoo bottle word
72 Victor Laszlo's wife
76 Light bulb, for Linus or Lucy

77 Back talk
79 Chat-room chortle
80 Street or squeeze starter
81 ___ Dame
83 Gets in with a crowbar
86 "Jackie Brown" star Pam
87 Bikini Bottom locale
88 Utility consumption
89 Become conscious of
90 Procures the hard way
91 Lab rats run them

DOWN

1 Senegal capital
2 Chico's chum
3 They smell
4 Risked getting bleeped
5 Prominent period
6 Conductor Kostelanetz
7 Drop-leaf table
8 Put away a dish
9 Become insipid
10 Upper New York Bay island
11 Tilly in "The Big Chill"
12 Lost traction on a wet road
13 Honeymoon rooms
14 Hawk's hook
15 Grabbed some shut-eye
20 Storm cloud
25 Sire, in the Scriptures
29 Operetta with Nanki-Poo

31 Signaler of 61 Across
33 "Independence Day" ships
35 Opportunity for a station break?
37 Having a harsh tone
38 Hang in the air
39 Protein acid
41 Crusoe's creator
42 Dispatch
43 "Oh, hush up!"
44 Experimented with
45 Surgery souvenirs
47 Biblical antitheses of swords
52 Centers of activity
53 MRI predecessor
55 Kind of basin
57 Sock pattern
59 Fish-fowl go-between

60 He goes postal?
65 Champagne/orange juice drink
66 First Oscar-winning film
67 Regard devotedly
68 Begin to prevail
69 "America's movable fighting man"
71 Masters Brooklynese?
73 Bolivia's most populous city
74 Relentless attack
75 Meara and Murray
78 Magpie genus
82 In advance of, in verse
84 Mal de ___
85 Monetary amount

8 MAKING ENDS MEET   by Harvey Estes
42 Across may be one way to make ends meet . . . although it doesn't pertain here.

ACROSS

1 Flipped out
7 She walked into Rick's "gin joint"
11 Stock-in-___
16 Drill directive
17 Do or so
18 Blood component
19 Rub the wrong way
20 Checked item
21 Zimbalist in "The F.B.I."
22 Shut down bus station?
25 Basque terrorist org.
26 Keebler cookie maker
27 Health plan from 10 Down
28 Sine and cosine
30 Chesterfield et al.
33 Holds title to
35 Bywords
38 He cared for Samuel
40 Kind of base
42 Penny-pinching
43 Prom dress material
47 Electrical pain reliever
49 Skyrocket
50 Sapporo sash
51 Pointer from a pitching coach?
54 Historian Hoogenboom
55 Coventry containers
57 Queen Rania's predecessor
58 Deerstalker feature
60 Chihuahua "ciao"
62 1944 turning point
64 Thou of thous
65 Landlord
67 Jubilation
69 Tenor Lanza
73 Mann of education
75 ___ gratia artis
77 Surrey loc.
78 Priest's garment
80 Block a split end?
84 Filmy fabric
86 Mortgage claim
87 On the go
88 Riverbank romper
89 Infinitive with a circumflex
90 Luther's 95
91 Barely make it
92 Antarctic explorer Richard
93 "Three's Company" actress

DOWN

1 Takes a stab at
2 Verdi opera
3 Ignited
4 Makes lace
5 Land in water
6 Comb projections
7 Chic clique
8 Hover threateningly
9 Part of a flight
10 John Hancock rival
11 J. Alfred Prufrock's creator
12 TKO caller
13 Police quota?
14 Shared air
15 Flaubert heroine
23 Punk music genre
24 Chase robot
29 Williams of the Temptations
31 Yanks of 1917
32 Whole lot
34 Nonsynthetic
36 Butler's love
37 Variety of poker
39 Pack ___ (give up)
41 Get the pot going
43 Bottom line
44 Stomach
45 Take the last puff?
46 "And giving ___, up the chimney . . ."
48 "The King and I" setting
52 "Gunsmoke" setting
53 Ever so proper
56 Fair to middling
59 Lake Okeechobee loc.
61 Pishogue
63 Had a craving
66 Fan sound
68 It may come before long
70 Alter
71 "This is outrageous!"
72 Shrek's girlfriend
74 Paparazzi target
76 Skedaddles
78 Enthralled
79 After curfew
81 "From Here to Eternity" actress
82 Canyon sound
83 Tabloid twosome
85 Grandpa Walton

9 UP THE CORPORATE LADDER by Charles E. Gersch

Matthew Broderick starred in the award-winning 1995 revival of 18 Across.

ACROSS

1 Animal track
6 "New York Times" section
11 Cheerful adventure
15 **Author of 18 Across**
17 Suspicious smell
18 **1961 Broadway musical (with 49-A and 81-A)**
19 Asian desert expanse
20 Watering aid
21 Sci-fi baddie, often
22 Occupational hazard for supermodels?
24 1996 campaign name
26 Suffix akin to -ette
28 Like krypton
29 "Iron Man" Ripken
32 Norm's never-seen wife on "Cheers"
34 1989 Gregory Hines film
36 Domicile for Miss Piggy
37 Extirpates
39 "Porgy and Bess" character ___ Life
43 Shade of yellow
44 Lucy without a née?
45 "Cope Book" author Bombeck
49 **See 18 Across**
52 Right on the map
53 Chris of Coldplay
54 Indited
55 Cook wear?
57 Cooks slowly
58 FDR power project
61 ___ Anne de Beaupré
62 Roulette bet
64 Former British Airways jet
65 Goes overboard
67 Light setting
70 Meryl's "Holocaust" role
72 Pacific weather phenomenon
74 Site of Italy's Mangia Tower
76 Bones of Sleepy Hollow
80 Azure
81 **See 18 Across**
84 Shakespearean royal
85 **Composer of 18 Across**
86 Sushi seafood
87 Confronts
88 Valentine's Day gift

DOWN

1 "Scat, cat!"
2 Rows for the religious
3 Chose
4 "So that's it!"
5 Flea market offerings, e.g.
6 Year when Shakespeare turned 37
7 Man with a mike
8 Second-decaders
9 Dawn Chong in "The Alibi"
10 Track info
11 Boston airport
12 Goes ape over
13 **Morse who starred in 18 Across**
14 McNichol of "Family"
15 "Quiet!"
16 Stick in school
23 Amerind abode: Var.
25 Pizzeria needs
27 Thrown (about)
29 "The Color Purple" heroine
30 Fight site
31 Animals lost in song
33 Toward the back
35 Town in central Italy
38 Dixie
40 Mail from Paris
41 Type of inspection
42 Late-1960s jacket
44 Trapped
46 Book about Kunta Kinte's family
47 Trombone attachments
48 "This is only ___ . . ."
50 Not an orig.
51 Nasal sound
56 Gp. or org.
57 Kyl or Kohl, e.g.
58 Threefold
59 **Rudy who costarred in 18 Across**
60 Forget-me-not, e.g.
63 Tough plastic
66 Stadium sections
68 Pitman of shorthand
69 Tigger's creator
71 Bottomless pit
73 "Carmina Burana" composer
75 Part of BPOE
77 Angry reaction
78 Cash-register stack
79 Bus. executive
82 A time to remember
83 Stutz Bearcat rival

10 NOTED EMBELLISHMENTS   by John Underwood

Combine prefixes of 19-A, 34-A, and 64-A to 50-A for the fancy names of 83-A.

ACROSS

1 Treaty
5 Peruvian pals
11 Agglomerate
16 Lysol target
17 Once in a blue moon
18 Civic model
19 United Airlines magazine
21 Union station
22 Curb
23 "GQ" publisher Condé
24 Court tie
25 Flibbertigibbet
28 Ovine parent
30 They're reputed to come from Mars
31 Mystery woman
34 Zola's Nana, for one
37 Tognazzi in "La Cage aux Folles"
38 Bandy
40 On the move
41 Skin: Comb. form
43 Cardigan Bay, e.g.
45 "I ___ do just that!"
49 Body starter
50 Trembles
53 Southern sib
54 Place
56 Milk whey
57 ThinkPads
58 Saw
61 River of Flanders
63 Big Board newbie
64 Penultimate competition
68 Plum liqueur
70 Row in 71 Across
71 ___-tac-toe
72 Investment returns
74 "___ intended"
76 Itinerary listings
78 Low-budget prefix
82 Odette's alter ego
83 ___ notes
86 Flimflams
87 Spotted wildcat
88 Sink in
89 Whence riseth the phoenix
90 Forward
91 Cognizant of

DOWN

1 "Gateway" author Frederik
2 Chick trailer
3 Deep sleep
4 "Valse ___": Sibelius
5 Sculptor from Strasbourg
6 ___-jongg
7 Name meaning "peace"
8 Baritone role in "Andrea Chénier"
9 Bullying salvos?
10 Routines
11 College life
12 Inside man
13 Third of a Vivaldi four
14 ___-out (dazed)
15 Composed
20 Deep-bodied herrings
26 Neanderthal man feature
27 Reeves in "Johnny Mnemonic"
29 Punster
31 Apostle replaced by Matthias
32 Broker
33 180° from sud
35 Trattoria
36 Spike-horned antelope
39 Need of some banks
42 "Gateway of the Americas"
44 Allhallows' ___
46 Top dog
47 Allegretto and prestissimo
48 "Ender's Game" author ___ Scott Card
51 Ballet ___ de Monte Carlo
52 Whiff
55 Insanity
59 Midnight for Minerva
60 Beaver tooth
62 Agnes de Mille ballet
64 Neighbor of Chihuahua
65 Old Testament book
66 In the dumps
67 Catamounts
69 100 centavos, once
73 Agave fiber
75 Jackson played by Fonda
77 Matisse slept here
79 Setting of "The Plague"
80 Food packaging abbr.
81 Speedskater Apolo
84 Thither
85 Bouquet bringer

11 TOY BOX by Diane Epperson

A recent visit to Fifth Avenue's FAO Schwarz store inspired this theme.

ACROSS

1 Dogie catcher
6 Lockboxes
11 DA's aide
15 Break up, informally
16 Used a prie-dieu
17 Heads of France
19 "I've been to the ___...": M.L. King
21 Play ground
22 Like springtime trees
23 [Not my error]
24 Spinning one's wheels
25 Asian occasion
26 Dot follower
28 Diamonds, e.g.
30 "___ life!"
31 Comic-strip device
34 Type of pig or stove
37 Zhou ___
38 Shock jock of talk radio
39 Refrain syllable
41 Asimov classic
45 Parking place
46 Flag with three crosses
50 ___ roll (lucky)
51 "Mona Lisa" home
53 Flop
54 Telltale sign
55 "... and not ___ to drink"
58 Leftovers container
61 "Die Fledermaus" highlight
65 Felipe or Moises of baseball
66 Ratio phrase
67 British recording co.
68 Carte start
71 Like a cube
73 Balin in "The Black Orchid"
75 Bead counter
77 Crowning glory?
78 Memory snag
80 Diamond flaw
81 Studio sign
82 Like a ghost ship
83 Hardy heroine
84 Between moorings
85 Get more "Time"

DOWN

1 Send money
2 "___ ear and out..."
3 Mature
4 Prong
5 Embassy staffer
6 Manage moguls
7 Sheridan and Sothern
8 Talisman
9 Harangue
10 "Racer's edge" at Indy
11 ___ all-time high
12 Ladies' room?
13 Bose product
14 Note held for the full count
18 Lucifer
20 "___ and his money..."
24 Emphatic type
27 Prefix for media
29 Faisal ___ Abdul Aziz
31 Atlanta station
32 Greek sandwich
33 Small songbird
34 Bolus
35 Melville work
36 1984 Nobelist for Peace
40 What's more
42 Tinseltown turkey
43 Fit for duty
44 Sharp taste
46 Pakistani language
47 Sea nymph
48 Law in "The Aviator"
49 Pueblo material
52 Dallas cowboys
54 Olive ___
56 Hosp. areas
57 Like Job
59 ___ Abdel Nasser
60 More fluent
61 Lusterless surface
62 "Cotton Candy" trumpeter
63 Jimmy Dorsey hit
64 Fargo and Summer
68 Scrat's "Ice Age" quest
69 Desi's daughter
70 Out of whack
72 Canal zones?
74 Play to ___ (draw)
76 Helm position
78 Extinct New Zealander
79 Basso Berberian

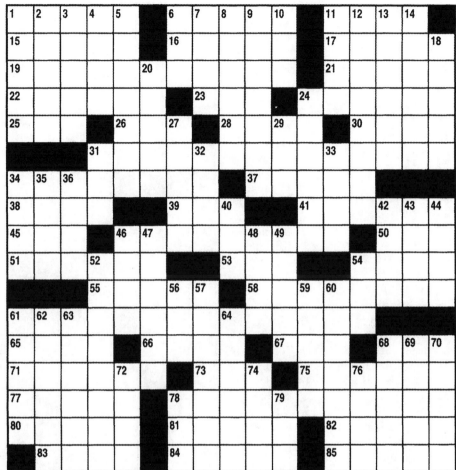

12 "I GET AROUND"   by Norman S. Wizer
Don't be fooled by the title, there isn't one Beach Boys clue below.

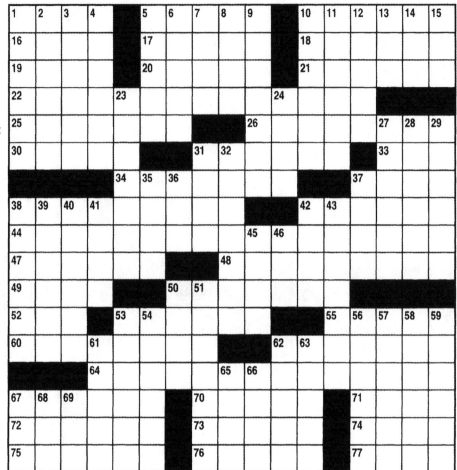

ACROSS

1 Lieut.
5 Conspirator with Brutus
10 Levitra rival
16 It's a wrap
17 Gussy up
18 "Upon my oath!"
19 ATF agent
20 Namby-pamby
21 Took a weekender out
22 **Start of a Steven Wright observation**
25 Put a new label on
26 Cattle farmer
30 URL mark
31 Father of Xerxes
33 Make ___ of it
34 Sea salt
37 "Don't have ___, man!": Simpson
38 Trevor Immelman's 2005 Masters feat
42 "___-Boom-Der-E"
44 **Middle of observation**
47 Put on the bulletin board again
48 Burgeons
49 Mixture
50 Bullring figure
52 Bar degree
53 Residents of Tara
55 "We ___ please!"
60 Separate
62 Lady of Livorno
64 **End of observation**
67 Kelso's owner
70 Of the hip bone
71 "The joke's ___!"
72 1999 U.S. Open winner
73 Watch brand
74 A stone's throw away
75 Domestic-sci class
76 Pool employee
77 Beach birds

DOWN

1 Hunt and Peck
2 Barber or Butler
3 Greek city-state
4 Where to raise a racket
5 Quibble
6 Words of wisdom
7 Future jr.
8 Neonate's bed
9 Pyrenees republic
10 Trimurti member
11 Hull and Hayes
12 The Make-___ Foundation
13 Salon dollop
14 Arctic explorer
15 Dull ending
23 Cultural groups
24 Cloudburst
27 Showy parrots
28 Greek marketplaces
29 "Not on your life!"
31 Power: Comb. form
32 Vespucci namesake
35 "Such ___ is Rosalinde": Shak.
36 Remote button
37 Quarter
38 Lloyd in "The Freshman"
39 Spots on a peacock's tail
40 Fats
41 Buck ending
42 Rookie: Var.
43 Par for the course
45 Genetic fingerprints
46 Date-stamped: Abbr.
50 "___-cake baker's man . . ."
51 Peacemaking
53 City NW of Madrid
54 Tempestuous
56 Vocalize
57 He butted out?
58 President from Missouri
59 A big part of Wayne's world?
61 Selected
62 Cleaners' concern
63 Inuit home
65 Line above the equator: Abbr.
66 River to the Seine
67 "Well, lah-di-___!"
68 Tognazzi in "La Cage aux Folles"
69 Spray grease

13 THE NEW MUNSTERS   by Jay Hackney

72 Across was also a member of the 5th Dimension vocal group.

ACROSS

1 Christmas trees
5 They're flowerless and rootless
11 Harry Potter's forte
16 Capital on the Red Sea
17 Green on bronze
18 Wound the pride of
19 NASA scrub
20 "Hee Haw" banjoist
22 Siamese scratchers
24 Hearst's abductors, briefly
25 Porous scrubbers
26 "Nine to Five" star
29 Kind of school
30 Israeli firearm
31 Avails oneself of
32 Long fish
34 High-arcing shot
37 Sitcom veteran Arthur
38 Cacophony
39 Turn into a parking lot
40 Inevitable outcome
41 Dead heat
42 "Que" follower in song
43 Paddle one's own ___
44 WW1 flying ace
49 Butcher shop cuts
50 Insensitive sort
51 Dorothy Parker trait
52 Squarish
53 Arachnid on a dust speck
54 Take part in a demolition derby
55 "I've found you out!"
58 Buddy, to Balzac
59 Pear named after a Belgian
60 Melt meat
61 British isle
62 GNP topic
64 "The Caine Mutiny" author
67 Approaches aggressively
70 NASCAR circuit?
71 Pay (out)
72 "Solid Gold" cohost (1981–84)
75 1968 award for Al Pacino
76 Devoid of meaning
77 Away from home
78 Rave partner
79 Muddle-minded
80 Like boxing gloves
81 Millipede's multitude

DOWN

1 Groupie group
2 Adore unquestion-ingly
3 Finery
4 Pleasing to ski lodge owners
5 Fuel-efficiency stat
6 Coxswain's crew
7 Plays for time
8 Egyptian peninsula
9 Discontinua-tion
10 Drains (strength)
11 Burns and Houlihan, on "M*A*S*H"
12 ". . . to get her poor dog ___"
13 Way off a ship
14 Comprehending comment
15 Luck of the Irish
21 Waldorf salad fruit
23 Examines in detail
27 Basketry twig source
28 Not as distant
33 Hunter who wrote as Ed McBain
35 Nebraska county
36 Homer's favorite is Duff
39 Teahouse order
40 Encyclopedia tidbit
41 Lilliputian
42 Rob Roy ingredient
43 South American crocodilians
44 Napoleon's 1814 address
45 Ensure the failure of
46 Gov. Thurmond in 1948
47 Hieroglyphics bird
48 Safari boss
53 "Zonk" purveyor Hall
54 Leo McKern's TV barrister
55 Unicellular swimmers
56 Semi purpose
57 Short socks
59 Tom on "Happy Days"
60 Found the source of
63 Numismatist's display
65 Rodrigo Díaz de Vivar
66 Fingerprint feature
67 Enclosed by
68 "Will you allow me?"
69 Go ape
73 Museum curator's deg.
74 IOOF member?

HAPPINESS IS . . . by Monica Brenner
A humorous quote from the unforgettable Uncle Miltie.

ACROSS

1 To-go order
6 High-five
10 Stuffed shirt
14 Pen sound
17 Dante's "La vita ___"
18 RPM indicator
19 Immaculate
20 Like this clue: Abbr.
21 **Start of a Milton Berle quote**
23 Assailant
25 Lexicon
26 Benchmark
28 Eta follower
29 "Alligator" shirt company
30 "For that's the golden mark ___ to hit": Shak.
32 Yours, in Tours
33 **More of quote**
38 Tie score
39 It lacks refinement
40 Sycophants
41 Grain holders
42 Winter woe
44 Nouveau ___
47 Three dots, in Morse
48 Charge
49 Skewbald or piebald
51 Fauna's partner
53 **More of quote**
59 Sight from Everest
60 Mary ___ (Innes ship)
61 Skater Kulik
62 Soft shoe
65 "Here's ___, Mrs. Robinson . . ."
67 Indiana Jones quest
68 Arnaz and son
69 Beethoven's third
71 Accomplished
73 Nymph once married to Paris
74 **More of quote**
79 Black: Comb. form
80 Was busy at a bee
81 Lil ___ (Derby winner)
82 "What's ___ like?"
84 Lunar ring
85 Price lines?
90 Sha Na Na members, slangily
92 **End of quote**
94 "___ for Evidence": Grafton
95 Langston Hughes poem
96 Gold: Comb. form
97 Acrylic fiber
98 Teriyaki ingredient
99 ___ Féin
100 "___ joy keep you . . .": Sandburg
101 Up the ante

DOWN

1 Catch a liner
2 Pick out
3 Hershey candy
4 Rara ___
5 Palatial estates
6 Solid alcohol
7 Royal bride of 1981
8 One of five in "Hamlet"
9 More affected
10 Trunk items
11 Sangaree spice
12 Leftover
13 Fatigued
14 Squeeze in a schedule
15 Paint solvents
16 Brings before the bench
22 Rapper who founded NWA
24 Gabs
27 Dogwood relative
31 Peep site
33 Join up
34 Sam in "Wimbledon"
35 Miscellaneous collection of goods
36 Wellspring
37 Mule chasers
38 Septa plus one
42 Jeff in "Icon"
43 Deceive verbally
45 ". . . that which ___ prove false!": Shak.
46 Work in sales
49 Torpedo ships
50 Seminary degree
52 ___ generis (of another kind)
54 Abercrombie's partner
55 Check the math
56 Nancy in "Sunset Blvd."
57 In competition
58 Assuage
62 Mixtures
63 "The Messiah" is one
64 Politesse
66 Arizona statesman (1922–98)
68 Smoke alarm
70 Jim Croce's "___ Name"
72 All in all
73 New Mexico county
75 "Bewitched" (2005) director
76 Rationality
77 Jay or Lionel of golf
78 Livorno locale
83 Medical suffix
86 Other, in Oviedo
87 Grocery section
88 Son of Zeus
89 New Year's Eve word
91 Wormhole traveler
93 Color gradation

15 BEATIFIC BEGINNINGS   by Patrick Jordan
Mr. Philips should appreciate the alternative music clue at 31 Down.

ACROSS

1 Mussolini's movement
8 Brought dishonor upon
14 Horror author Stoker
18 Shrinking Asian lake
19 Siesta shawl?
20 Initiation, e.g.
21 The flag of England
23 Radar enigmas
24 Blubbering bead
25 Olive-hued songbirds
26 "The Girl From ___" (1964 hit)
28 Specify
30 Hammerlock target
31 A-listers
32 "Fanny" writer Jong
34 1985 Brat Pack film
38 Carnivorous zodiac sign
39 Spendthrift's jag
42 Skye in "Stranded"
43 Carder's concern
45 Hostile kind of "sandwich"
47 Cable modem alternative
49 TV fare
52 Far from fantastic
53 Mouths
55 TIROS-launching org.
58 Mother Hubbard, e.g.
59 When some march in March
63 Like a julep
66 Scholarship basis
67 "How was ___ know?"
68 Jab
72 Potemkin Mutiny site
74 Badminton barrier
76 Add software
78 Kite type
79 Parquetry piece
82 Dissonant
84 Hobby shop buy
85 Klamath weed
89 Acts as a lookout, say
91 In the offing
92 Ticket number
93 Consort of Cronus
94 Soft sheepskin leather
97 Home of the nene
99 For each
102 Move quickly
103 Vatican City entrance
106 Mrs. Charles Lindbergh
107 Brat
108 Indifferent
109 Cattail or bamboo
110 Defies the censor
111 Railroad bridge

DOWN

1 Skip supper
2 Commedia dell'___
3 Acutely discerning
4 Ordainee
5 Seeking, in the personals
6 Start a volleyball game
7 Crèche trio
8 Declared forcefully
9 Look flattering on
10 Some LAX postings
11 ___ Tomé and Príncipe
12 Greek consonant
13 Can't stomach
14 Its capital is Bandar Seri Begawan
15 Abounding (with)
16 Fission particle
17 Butte's kin
22 Delete from a disk
27 Treasury Dept. bureau
29 Burdensome bit of work
31 Punk music genre
32 Lodge with a Grand Exalted Ruler
33 City that aptly rhymes with "casino"
35 Purple shade
36 "Seabiscuit" scene
37 Bruisable traits
40 Alka-Seltzer jingle word
41 Aired again
44 Memorable pair?
46 Sells for
48 Derogatory
50 Nancy's "Rhoda" role
51 Romantic rendezvous
54 Made a meal of
56 Emulate Bode Miller
57 Exhibiting activity
60 Country singers England and Herndon
61 Ask for more "Money"
62 Clothes oneself in
63 Crowd around
64 Wedding vows
65 "Whose turn for service?"
69 Disassemble
70 Came to rest
71 Short orders?
73 They haven't a prayer
75 Boomerang users
77 Imperial Iranian
80 Highly agitated
81 Tripper's hallucinogen
83 Battling
86 Sat in with a jazz band
87 Exultation exclamation
88 Soapbox occupant
90 Brilliant examples, slangily
93 Choir platform
94 Powerful businessperson
95 Make keener
96 Unbeatable rating
97 Mount Olympus queen
98 "___ She Lovely": Wonder
100 Paperless exam
101 Mauna Loa goddess
104 Historic beginning?
105 What, to Juan

16 ANIMAL HOUSE   by Matt Skoczen
Many critics feel 17 Across deserved an Oscar nomination for that performance.

ACROSS

1 Cairo cobras
5 Dejected sound
9 Doorway components
14 MSN competitor
17 Giamatti in "Sideways"
18 Frogner Park site
19 Circe's island
20 '80s antimissile program
21 "Green Hills of Africa" author
24 Hawaiian hawks
25 Give ___ (cause)
26 More chilling
27 Don't pay this for a new car: Abbr.
28 Western Samoan currency
30 Paycheck abbr.
31 "Desperate Housewives" character
33 Sylvan deity
36 Same old, same old
41 Wolfman Jack spun them
42 Weekly program
44 Med. specialist
45 "South Park" brother
46 River to the Caspian
48 Prospector's find
49 Cut-up
51 Reverend in "Emma"
53 Colorado and Kansas
55 Elixir
57 Comedy show that spawned "Happy Days"
63 "Brave New World" caste
64 TV "Mission: Impossible" leader
66 Military student
69 Strong alkali
70 Granny
73 Suggestive
74 Turkish leader
75 Ailing
77 New Testament book
79 Jamaica "gent"
80 "Per ardua ad astra" org.
84 Egg-shaped
86 Gusted
87 Diner dinner
88 Faction
90 Alcohol in fusel oil
92 Black teas
94 "War of the ___" (2005)
98 Buddy's hillbilly role
99 Pirate phrase
102 Jehoshaphat's father
103 Japanese immigrant
104 Nefarious
105 Mideast port
106 2004 Jamie Foxx film
107 Polish ruling house of yore
108 Derivative of Helen
109 Puts in carpets

DOWN

1 Mimic
2 Wrap on a rani
3 Crossword humor
4 Like a cold shower?
5 Yucca-like plant
6 Suffix for shrew
7 Jubilation
8 Out of jeopardy
9 Muppet band member
10 Sea off Greece
11 Bryn ___
12 Actress Benaderet
13 For instance
14 "Let me tell you . . ."
15 Polecat's protection
16 Baby talk
22 Dallas hockey team
23 Lily and crocus
27 DI doubled
29 Soil: Comb. form
31 Tyrol trailer
32 Muppet bandleader
33 Tipsy talk
34 Keep America Beautiful month
35 National Park of Kenya
37 Financial ___
38 Not a meat eater
39 "Love ___": Pendergrass
40 Hunger
43 Martinelli and Schiaparelli
47 Flood defense
49 UTEP's league
50 Airline to Tokyo
52 Stratum
54 Chameleon, e.g.
55 Brooch
56 Hill channel
58 Prefix for meter
59 English cathedral town
60 Shad delicacy
61 Alpaca relative
62 Disney World area
65 Auld lang ___
66 Mini Cooper, for one
67 Back in time
68 "Godspell" song
70 Noted seafarers
71 ABC soap opera, briefly
72 Dundee denials
76 Murphy's ___
77 Autogyro part
78 Sin city
81 Tie word
82 "Constantine" star
83 Put on an act
85 Viva-voce
89 Beatles song
90 Open a bit
91 Phoenix suburb
92 City on the Arno
93 Golfer Ballesteros
95 "___ and the Swan": Yeats
96 Squirrel's nest
97 Nine-digit IDs
99 Taste
100 Philosopher Chu ___
101 Up to

GO FOR IT   by Bernice Gordon

"Ambition is a dream with a V8 engine." — Elvis Presley

ACROSS

1 Lascivious
5 Home to a señora
9 Moniker
13 "Ring My Bell" singer Anita
17 Be distressed
18 Redolence
19 Poet of ancient Rome
20 Double curve
21 **Start of an Abraham Lincoln quote**
24 Heckle
25 Equestrian
26 Once in a blue moon
27 Freshet
28 "Nothing doing"
29 Former GM line
30 Clump of earth
31 Stanza with four four-foot lines
35 **More of quote**
40 Multitude
41 Hen's home
42 Fit to devour
43 Hebrew month
44 Salary
45 Not up
47 Artist Bonheur
48 Greatest
50 Where Pan was worshiped
53 Shaggy ox
54 **More of quote**
57 Bowling Green conf.
60 Courtroom compensation
61 Unbecoming trait
65 Actress Nazimova
67 Brown or Fey
68 Balaam's mount
69 Pro ___
70 Implement
72 Short newspaper piece
74 Curry spice
75 **More of quote**
78 Paul Newman movie
79 Fury
80 Impetuous ardor
81 Make a purchase
82 Unpolished
85 Tiff
86 Garbage ___
91 Munich money
92 **End of quote**
94 Make an impression?
95 "The Hippopotamus" poet
96 "Bring It on Home ___": Cooke
97 Pork cut
98 Gaelic
99 "___ All Laughed": Gershwin
100 Was in debt
101 Makes a selection

DOWN

1 Plaster backing
2 Sonic return
3 Buzzing sound
4 Leonine abodes
5 Universal
6 Spiral-horned antelope
7 Coming up
8 Pinball path
9 Wandering tribes
10 Loath
11 Tiny pest
12 Conductor de Waart
13 One ended in November 1918
14 Exchange premium
15 Give a new look to
16 Quitclaim
22 Bottled-up one?
23 Warship deck
27 Pay (the bill)
29 "My goodness!"
30 Nuances
31 Attention getter
32 "Shark Tale" dragonfish
33 Nitty-gritty
34 Emcee's forte
35 Play around (with)
36 Most in need of herbicide
37 "About ___" (Hugh Grant film)
38 "As Time Goes By" requester
39 Boat wood
41 Medicinal tea
44 Regarded as such
45 Book of the Bible
46 Expletive from Scrooge
49 Aftermath of a heavy rain
50 Pond life
51 City on Long Island Sound
52 Past
55 Woods of "China Beach"
56 Play a guitar
57 Handle roughly
58 Der ___ (Adenauer)
59 Musical sign
62 Poetic foot
63 Cookbook direction
64 Smarty Jones' hair
66 Counterpoison
68 Ready follower
71 Really riled
72 Speechify
73 ___ Homme Richard
74 Tropical rodent
76 Rest and relaxation
77 Razzle-dazzle
78 Still
81 Ecological community
82 Give up
83 One who feels remorse
84 Patio pots
85 Reza Pahlavi was one
86 Arabian sailboat
87 European capital
88 Word to brake for
89 Roosted
90 Fisheye ___
92 Implosion cause
93 It replaced GATT

18 "GIVE IT HERE!" by Raymond Hamel
Hilary Swank won an Oscar playing 104 Across.

ACROSS

1 Enamored with
7 1994 Dave Foley film
13 Greek island
18 Ethically neutral
19 Beefalo: Var.
20 Lebanon president Lahoud
21 Recurrence observation*
23 Bumper sticker
24 Quick cut
25 Infuriated
26 "CSI: Miami" is one
28 German article
29 Digs in
31 Andress in "Dr. No"
33 "The Duchess of ___": Goya
34 Calibration guide*
39 Flow regulator*
43 Osamu Tezuka cartoon character
44 Like many Hawaiian flowers
45 Space chimp of 1961
48 Take a job
49 Set off
51 Thailand, previously
54 "___ Romano" (2001)
55 Maine resort*
58 Star
63 Author Dinesen
64 Like private lessons
70 Egyptian deity
72 Throneberry of baseball
74 Naturally picturesque
75 Its flag features a bison
78 Fierstein's Trilogy*
80 Sad Sack's rank*
83 Otolaryngology concerns
84 Official emissary
85 Weathercock
86 Former warrior
89 Mexican-American
93 Less than enthusiastic
95 Opera with elephants
96 Race with batons
97 "$10,000 Pyramid" category/ start of CLUE* ANSWERS
101 She played Granny on TV
102 Grow fainter
103 Frittata
104 Maggie Fitzgerald, e.g.
105 Has desires
106 Nuisance

DOWN

1 Not so
2 Musandam peninsula dweller
3 Lose-lose
4 Go down
5 Clumsy one
6 Jeb Bush's st.
7 Bakery men
8 Gerald O'Hara's plantation
9 Stone likeness
10 Beeping sources
11 Nut-brown brew
12 Some College Bowl questions
13 Like Spock's advice
14 "I agree!"
15 "Miami Vice" cop
16 Lemony Snicket's evil count
17 Women's magazine
22 Of utmost importance
27 Poet married to Ted Hughes
29 Jones of the John Coltrane Quartet
30 1981 hit album for Genesis
32 RR stop
33 Saxophone range
34 X
35 Picador's target
36 Hair stylist José
37 Kasparov's end man
38 ZIP code 10001 locale
39 Clamming area
40 Berserker's weapon
41 Auction unit
42 Changes direction
46 1970 World's Fair site
47 ___ Bors de Ganis
50 Mai ___
52 From the start
53 Cal. column heading
56 Ark son
57 Read again
58 Purse item
59 Ishmael's son-in-law
60 Hayes of "The Mod Squad"
61 "___ the Viking" (1989)
62 Extra
65 Yellow orange, in Yorkshire
66 "The Untouchables" leader
67 Lennon's second wife
68 "Little Birds" author Anaïs
69 Ticker tape?
71 Kierkegaard
73 Part of some RFD addresses
76 Bias
77 Gardner in "Lone Star"
79 Prepared
81 "Dog Day Afternoon" chant
82 New driver, often
85 Clamping tools
86 Medical containers
87 1959 Ranger hardtop
88 Common sense?
89 Tot's bed
90 Beau ideal
91 Holly genus
92 Walking aid
94 PC key
95 Men behaving badly
98 Haw preceder
99 Sound of delight
100 John's "Be Cool" costar

19 WRITER'S BLOC   by John Greenman
The clue at 13 Down is an example of a tautonym.

ACROSS

1 Evian and Vichy
5 Vega, for one
9 First MoMA director
13 Young bull
17 Kelp, e.g.
18 Turner in "Betrayed"
19 Back talk?
20 Blue Bonnet, for one
21 Dupe Thomas?
23 Mouthful for Robert?
25 Most snappish
26 Hall-of-Famer Traynor
27 Broadcast
28 Slangy negative
29 Help with a heist, e.g.
31 Tickled pink
35 Cringe in fear
38 Aphrodite's son
39 Leonine retreat
40 Chinese creative principle
41 Mount Rushmore face
42 Played
44 Bridle straps
45 CIA forerunner
46 Edwin Drood's fiancée
48 Thomas' goatee?
50 Patella site
51 Pensioner
53 Appends
54 Pays attention to
55 ___ fixe (obsession)
56 Pandemonium
58 Prospect
59 Brightest star in Cygnus
61 Highlands hillside
62 Landfill concern
65 Automotive pioneer
66 Ezra's birthday fare?
69 Thick slice
70 Mai ___ (rum drink)
71 Like some gas heaters
72 Brioche ingredient
74 Women's ___
75 Basque separatist group
76 Peerage member
77 Designer's tack
78 Caesurae
80 Tearing apart
82 Tenor Borgioli
83 Mongrel
84 "___ Paloma Blanca"
85 Wrigley field?
86 Gift recipient
90 Edgar's chamber?
94 George in a hurry?
96 Amo, amas, ___
97 The same: Lat.
98 Pitti Palace river
99 March slogan word
100 Agile
101 Lofty abode: Var.
102 Pear-shaped fruits
103 Absurdist movement

DOWN

1 Strongbox
2 Drudge
3 Wide-eyed
4 Like Sevier Lake
5 Diagonal
6 Strumpet
7 As well as
8 Sunbeam
9 Seem suitable for
10 Zoning unit
11 Plato's P
12 "As You Like It" heroine
13 Naja naja
14 Larter in "Legally Blonde"
15 Charter
16 Other side
22 "These Dreams" group
24 Torte layers, e.g.
26 Footlike part
29 Neck of the woods
30 Functional group
31 Braces
32 Irving's barriers?
33 Alleviated
34 Med nurse's concerns
35 Former KISS drummer Eric
36 Bassoon's kin
37 Nathaniel's tribesman?
38 Rochester's employee
39 Starring roles
43 Arch type
44 Decorate anew
47 Adjutants
49 Bleated
50 Salvages
52 Yank's foe
54 Shake a leg
56 Draconian
57 Bridge-game fourth
58 Nixonian signs
59 Mollycoddler
60 Buoy one's spirits
61 French market town
62 32-card game
63 Trot or canter
64 Diminishes
66 Flatworms
67 Greenish blue
68 Inflatable bed
71 Boxing fake
73 Large piece of luggage
77 Faint
79 Cleared a diskette
81 ___ miller (garden plant)
82 Tackling bag
83 Keeling Islands
85 Party ender
86 Metallic sound
87 Neighbor of Twelve Oaks
88 City WNW of Tulsa
89 Dame of comedy
90 Nitrous oxide, for one
91 Field-hockey official
92 Pitcher handle
93 "___ for Ted": Plath
94 Arabic letter
95 College in Little Rhody

20 HYBRID HUMOR   by Richard Silvestri
Talk about milking a joke!

ACROSS

1 Implore
8 Wildly enthusiastic
12 Silly smile
18 Kind of case
19 Occasion for proctors
20 Spicy cuisine
21 **Start of a quip**
24 Plains home
25 Honoree's place
26 Sweetie
27 FDR power project
28 24 mos. or more
29 Hung on to
30 In the center of
32 Shoe inserts
33 Teddy's cousin?
35 Shipshape
36 Carried
37 Father Sarducci
39 Wharton Sch. course
40 Compass drawing
41 **More of quip**
47 Like lager
48 Tale of adventure
49 500 place
50 Second-sequel designation
52 Auto pioneer Ransom
53 Lose luster
54 Aardvark's meal
55 Help a hood
56 Fruit center
57 Jai ___
58 Golden Fleece ship
59 Stroll
60 **More of quip**
64 Gradation of color
65 Speaker in Cooperstown
66 Fish stories
67 Take ___ (try)
70 Forum wear
71 Ballet studio fixture
73 Second-rank exec
74 Swiss river
75 Setting
76 Spill from a spile
79 One of Frank's exes
80 Gran Paradiso, e.g.
81 Hyalite
82 Don ___ de la Vega (Zorro)
84 **End of quip**
89 More bohemian
90 Pastrami preference
91 Plumber's need
92 Take the wrong way
93 Get into shape?
94 Special abilities

DOWN

1 Bananas
2 Old number?
3 Take them to act
4 Smooth sailing
5 "Look, Brutus!"
6 X, on a sweater
7 Paid attention to
8 See the point
9 Central line
10 Driving concern
11 Bill abbr.
12 Shore dinner entrée
13 Do a household chore
14 Julio, e.g.
15 Placard
16 Bankruptcy chapter
17 Change the postmark
22 Western wine valley
23 IOU
29 Drawer feature
30 Many millennia
31 1975 James Mason film
32 Central points
33 Docking areas
34 "___ late and a dollar short"
35 Final Four letters
36 Hinny's remark
37 Limerick language
38 Familiar with
39 Competitive advantage
40 Uses an abacus
42 Singer who won the Nobel prize
43 Heating or cooling device
44 Bruckner or Chekhov
45 Fair award
46 Gives way
47 Jazz style
51 Vulcan ending
53 Head for the hills
54 Son of Zeus and Hera
55 Dino's love
57 Border on
58 "Heat of the Moment" group
59 Seaweed substance
61 Smack
62 Primal impulse
63 Australia's largest lake
67 1975 Belmont winner
68 Difficult to endure
69 Red suit
70 GI lullaby
71 Bernard Goldberg book
72 Cry of relief
74 At the ready
75 Support the economy
76 Coupe kin
77 Scully or Mulder
78 Arthur and Elizabeth
80 Middle East gulf
81 Squashed circle
82 In two parts
83 Groundless
85 Never, in Neumünster
86 Massachusetts state tree
87 La Salle contemporary
88 PBS benefactor

21 PROCEED WITH CAUTION   by Ernest Lampert

Rearrange the circled letters in the grid to reveal the quip's author.

ACROSS

1 Does a boring job
6 "Miss Peaches" James of jazz
10 Some matériel
14 Channel for a '40s film
17 In reserve
18 Glassmaking oven
19 Former German capital
20 Zhou En-lai's successor
21 **Start of a quip**
24 Non-Rx
25 Icarus, briefly
26 Buddhist tower
27 "Two Gentlemen of Verona" dog
28 Famous "Tonight Show" tomahawk thrower
30 "The X-Files" org.
32 Roll call
33 Defunct mail center: Abbr.
36 Binary 7
37 Wiener roast side
39 Where hemoglobin is found
42 **More of quip**
43 Robert and Alan of films
44 Hipbone-related
46 Small dog
47 Kind of health coverage
49 American workers
54 Marathoner Pippig
55 Ars longa, ___ brevis
56 Picasso's model Maar
57 A Knute successor
58 Elixirs
61 **More of quip**
64 What Michelle Wie breaks
65 Nipped (with "out")
66 Buenos ___
67 **More of quip**
72 Engine cleaner
74 March Madness event
75 Super finish
76 Shaker ___, OH
77 River through Aragon

78 ___ avail (futile)
79 Gets one's goat
82 Source of linseed oil
83 Crescent-shaped
85 Polyester fabric
89 Fair and Milne
90 **End of quip**
93 Signature abbr.
94 Songstress Laine
95 Nagy of Hungary
96 Pond protozoan
97 Urchin's home
98 Pre-1991 Eurasian political divs.
99 Thessaly peak
100 Hayseed

DOWN

1 Mugs
2 Greek goddess of war
3 Kofi ___ Annan
4 Slalom champion Phil
5 Meteoric to the max
6 Cole Porter, the student
7 Fiesta Bowl site
8 Oakland nine
9 "To ___ and a bone . . .": Kipling
10 1984 Oscar-winning film
11 Protected sea mammal
12 Imaging test
13 Signs off on
14 "Civil Disobedience" essayist
15 Do the shag?
16 Duncan's murderer
22 Santa Fe, for one
23 Byzantine art form

27 Purity of a color
29 Citizen soldiers
31 "Let me say that again . . ."
33 Frame
34 Fronton ball
35 Third party, at times
37 Tar
38 No sound-alike
40 Pickup area
41 Casino lure
45 "___ Ding Dong Daddy From Dumas"
48 Pig out at a pig roast
49 Disseminated
50 Part of a downpayment, perhaps
51 Gung-ho
52 Most uninteresting
53 Gets smart
56 Buzz and butch
59 Est.

60 "High Hopes" lyricist
61 Bender
62 Elate
63 Take off
65 Emphatic refusal
67 Edberg and Zweig
68 Culpable
69 Huge land mass
70 Do a slow burn
71 Notes held to their full time value
73 Candy, for one
79 Mendeleev's study
80 Heads for
81 Jerk
84 Exchange fee
86 Offend olfactorily
87 "Eat ___ eaten!"
88 "The Subject Was Roses" star
90 Lt. factory
91 Bean and Cool J
92 Teachers' gp.

22 BUCKING THE CROWD by Rich Norris

"A literary classic is a book which people praise and don't read." — 69 Across

ACROSS

1 Military leaders
6 Visibly incredulous
11 They yield durable wood
18 Resulted in
19 Reds and Cards
20 ". . . but not ___ for tribute"
21 Basketry twig
22 Doughnut-shaped
23 Greyhound event
24 **Start of a quote**
27 Snorter starter?
28 Debtor's acknowledgment
29 Standoffish
30 Vitamin bottle no.
31 "Ronzoni ___ buoni . . ." (old ad jingle)
32 Fabric
35 **More of quote**
39 Restrain
42 Fresh
43 **More of quote**
46 Word puzzle
50 Grating sound
51 Novelist Paton
54 "Kid-tested, mother-approved" cereal
55 Apt. divisions
56 Gumby creator Clokey
57 **More of quote**
61 Book supplement: Abbr.
62 New Deal prog.
63 Music genre
64 Weigh-station factor
65 Ruins site near the Gulf of Salerno
66 PAC man
69 **Author of quote**
73 Family once called "landlords of New York"
75 Maker of the Fastskin suit
76 **More of quote**
80 1957 Tracy/Hepburn film
84 Seeding
85 Coastal eagle
86 Bourg's department
87 Ambient rocker Brian
88 They, in Tours
89 **End of quote**
95 Wear for a bank job
97 Humble spot
98 Dietary label
99 "I've been framed!"
100 Wine region near Bordeaux
101 Do a stand-up bit?
102 Ideas
103 Artery opener
104 Great czar

DOWN

1 Miss one's chance
2 Do a farrier job
3 French farewells
4 British machine gun
5 Peeved
6 Predate
7 Renown
8 High nest: Var.
9 Monastery
10 Old Portuguese coins
11 City SE of Milan
12 Bartlett's abbr.
13 Govt.-certified
14 "Bad Moon Rising" band, briefly
15 Find out about
16 Sally Ride's birthplace
17 Squash
25 Vividly green
26 Regional wildlife
31 Stone and Stallone
33 Three tsps.
34 Canton bordering Lake of Lucerne
36 "Gigli" heroine
37 Nautical pole
38 Strong glue
40 Good earth
41 Key of Beethoven's "Eroica"
43 Fish with a net
44 Silent screen star?
45 Abbr. followed by a date
47 Song syllables
48 JFK Library designer
49 D.C. broadcaster
52 1977 Steely Dan album
53 Expected outcomes
57 Assignation
58 René Préval's country
59 English Derby town
60 Harvest
65 Furry Lucas critter
67 Catch some rays
68 Joyce Kilmer poem
70 Prosecutor's privilege
71 City near Manchester, NH
72 P. Manning stats
74 Wading spots
76 Film effect akin to a "wipe"
77 Have a word with
78 Stand firm
79 Even if challenged
81 Deem appropriate
82 Sheathe
83 Reel
86 Accessory
89 ___ Alto
90 Comparative words
91 Luau lutes
92 Lymph ___
93 Scandal
94 Woodcraft, e.g.
96 Merry month in Paris

"SHOW SOME LEG!" by Manny Nosowsky
Tripod Trilogy: Part I

ACROSS

1 Rub elbows with
7 Rigatoni
12 More agile
18 Feature of Polyphemus
19 So all can hear
20 Links with
21 Intermediate position*
23 UFO pilots, e.g.
24 Annie's double?
25 Whitish hair*
27 Laugh-a-minute
29 Night hunter?
30 Work (out)
33 Six-packs for Muscle Beach?
36 Larry King's channel
37 Pay with plastic
40 Perfect places
41 Being blamed
44 It's on top of Old Smokey
45 Dismiss
46 Pépé le Moko's hideout
47 Mrs. Robinson's daughter
49 Gimlet or screwdriver
50 Spacemaker® microwaves
51 Bikini top
52 Metes out
53 Common background plot*
57 Tchaikovsky's "Eugene ___"
59 Stretch or stretch out
60 PA helpers
61 Came up in the world?
64 Voice box
65 Gains access online
67 Lacy mat
68 Grisly
69 One after the other
70 Use a thurible
71 "Don't just sit there!"
72 TV drama set in Vegas
74 Caduceus org.
75 Cloys
76 Spot for a sweater?
78 Ages and ages
80 23 Across, humorously*
86 Not worth a ___
89 Tabled, for now
90 Furniture and cars, GDP-wise*
93 Grand dam of Washington
94 Harangue
95 "Shark Tale" jellyfish
96 What waiters wait for
97 Chopper blade
98 "Si, si!"

DOWN

1 Directive for James?
2 "Door's open, come ___"
3 Nap sacks?
4 "Waking ___ Devine" (1998)
5 "Thimble Theatre" name
6 Road bug
7 Have a ball
8 Loads
9 Dybbuk, for one
10 Pull some strings?
11 Increase
12 No friend of the Czar
13 How to get in a heap of trouble?
14 It's the rule
15 WW1 flowing battle line
16 Pindar's "Pillar of heaven"
17 Looking good
22 Hoedown partner
26 Flatfoot's need?
27 Playground apparatus
28 ". . . ___ they say"
30 ___-tip pen
31 Prefix with gram or graph
32 "You have to move on!"
33 Pop-ups
34 Frank Fleer invention
35 It can be fixed
37 Side-order tidbit
38 Habit
39 Sheepish Ghanians?
41 Rapper born Tracy Marrow
42 With a twang
43 Hurt pride
44 Closeout crowd
47 Good listeners?
48 Law degree
50 Boomers' kids, for short
54 Tom Collins base
55 Flora and fauna
56 Blyth and others
57 Mezzo role in 57 Across
58 Drug cop
62 In addition
63 Slingshot forms
66 Mrs., abroad
67 Insecticide brand
69 Cherry variety
72 Telemarketer at work
73 Desert-boot leathers
75 Passed or past
76 Filched a fichu?
77 Enthusiasm
78 Bug-trapper in "Jurassic Park"
79 Bioelectric fish
80 Daft
81 "___ out, Bowser?"
82 Heavy thump
83 Drachma successor
84 Part of QED
85 Brussels-based alliance
86 Maker of CD players
87 Comics dog
88 Draws on
91 "Well, well, well"
92 Hosp. areas

ACROSS

1 "Thar she ___!"
6 Make red-faced
11 European economic union
18 Jeans fastener
19 Vascular trunk
20 Like Oedipus, at the end
21 Veterans' org. shakes into a made-in-USA Saturn?
23 Ring pro?
24 Canis and Felis, e.g.
25 Virtuous
26 Electra's brother
27 Hooch shakes into booze with a kick?
30 Sack for deliveries
35 QB goof
36 Mad Ave. world
41 Brown book shakes into a platinum McBeal?
44 Names names
47 Trained
48 Freshen a stamp pad
49 "___ Spiegel"
50 Small detail?
51 Béarnaise sauce ingredient
52 Like the Blue Ridge railway
54 Not fem. or neut.
56 "One" in a dog act
58 Worker with flowers
59 Pitt picture shakes into Genesis 3:23 and 3:24?
63 Once owned
66 Miracle-___ (plant food)
67 Town with an 800-year-old pueblo
68 Japanese "artisan"
72 Downwind, nautically
74 "Good heavens!"
76 Baseball's "Little Giant"
78 Internet business
79 Caffeine kick
80 ["You're cute, Elmer"]
81 "Tell it to the judge" shakes into a bar drink?
83 Electricity
85 Barker of Tarzan films
87 Everlasting
88 Harvestman shakes into lengthy paternity suits?
93 Profile feature
97 Lake discovered by Joliet
98 Analogize
104 "Marry ___, repent at . . ."
105 Class act shakes into a 1991 "Unforgettable" remake?
107 Milady's bedroom
108 "You've never ___ computer?"
109 Build on
110 Charge
111 Taken alone
112 Medicates

DOWN

1 Talk big
2 Whitewash ingredient
3 Home of Poppin' Fresh?
4 Number one starter?
5 Go in circles?
6 Mini-battery
7 A beatnik beats it
8 "What ___!" ("How funny!")
9 Singer without a song
10 Submit homework
11 Small, exquisite trinket
12 Mes in el año
13 Modern times, as an age
14 First Wives Club members
15 Light air
16 Movie nickname for Ulysses
17 Gen-___ (boomer's kids)
22 Group in a plot
28 "___, Our Help in Ages Past"
29 Cotton swab or rapper
30 Where Pathfinder landed
31 Guinness in "Kafka"
32 "Lady, shall ___ in your lap?": Shak.
33 Mrs. Cheney
34 Blues legend
37 High partner
38 Palindromic airhead
39 Between jobs
40 One of Auntie Em's farm hands
42 Pixar clownfish
43 Not keeping the breeze out
45 Not hearing
46 Scrawny animal
50 Anchovy group
53 Digital storage medium
55 Stop on a line: Abbr.
57 Steal wool?
60 Area near TriBeCa
61 Punta del ___, Uruguay
62 Came across by chance
63 Fifth Pillar of Islam
64 1966 NL batting champ
65 Where salamis hang
69 Faisal's predecessor
70 Al "He's the King" ___
71 Wynonna Judd's voice
73 And so forth
75 Jell-O form
77 High bell sound
81 Guns N' Roses lead singer
82 "Long time ___!"
84 Vitascope inventor
86 Binoculars accessory
89 Con men?
90 Tractor handle?
91 Crude carrier
92 Can't live without
93 Be in harmony
94 Strong as ___
95 Clobber
96 Put on hold?
99 Thigh muscle
100 Reverse
101 Helps
102 Carry
103 Adam's grandson
106 Little Rachel

25 "BREAK A LEG!" by Manny Nosowsky
Tripod Trilogy: Part III

ACROSS

1 In itself
6 Cuts short
10 Infield bounce
13 Two or three
17 Tool for Edmund Hillary
18 "___ Ordinary Man": Lerner & Loewe
19 Gloating cry
20 Junction
21 SCHOLASTIC . . .
22 . . . APTITUDE TESTS
24 Graph-paper feature
25 More cunning
26 Go for it
27 "Fiddlesticks!"
28 Reply to "Shall we?"
29 Goes quickly
31 Rhine maiden of myth
33 "Clever thought!"
36 Rhine maiden's frock
37 Missing link?
40 Holders of world views?
41 Fly catchers
42 Park place
44 Potbelly
45 Has a bug
46 "U.S. Male" singer
48 Rhine maiden's pronoun
49 Fur prized by royalty
51 Tab picker-uppers
52 FIGHT . . .
54 . . . SITE
55 Unlevel the playing field?
58 Crab
59 Jupiter is made of this
62 The Magi, notably
63 Rid of rind
64 Réne Préval's land
66 Bridge authority
67 Actions at chuck-a-luck
68 Drag out
70 "My God," in Hebrew
71 "The Rose of ___"

74 Locate and aim at
75 Judicial reference
77 G.D. of Metamucil fame
78 Pants part
80 Clear a building lot
81 "Gotcha!"
82 Briefly
86 Woodrow Wilson Guthrie's son
87 TOTAL . . .
89 . . . REFINEMENT
90 Bronze-casting oven
91 Hear here
92 Circus Circus sign
93 Snorkeler's heaven
94 Breed of terrier
95 Nincompoop
96 Flicker food
97 Not used to

DOWN

1 Short movies?
2 Environmental sci.
3 Have faith (with "on")
4 Where the price is right
5 Doctor's order
6 Large little piggies
7 Mario Puzo book
8 "___ in Black": Beatles
9 Nestlé's ___-Caps
10 Nightmare visions
11 "Too bad"
12 Used Usenet
13 Go fish
14 ITS SYMBOL IS THE . . .
15 Check text
16 Takes the plunge
23 Spur-of-the-moment comments
30 "Dejection: An ___" (Coleridge)

32 Big name in outdoor wear
33 Bags baddies
34 Needle case
35 HOW "PILGRIM'S PROGRESS" . . .
36 MEMBER OF VIRGINIA'S . . .
38 Maple genus
39 ___ Ed. class
41 Chicanery
43 Cornerstone abbr.
45 Up to it
46 Gym ball
47 Extend a tour of duty
49 Overhead light
50 PIN points?
51 Dead on target
52 Expose
53 Double-0 men
54 Shaggy dog's story?
55 Storm
56 Graven image

57 . . . SHOULD BE READ
58 . . . LOWER HOUSE
59 . . . KÉPI BLANC
60 "___ extra cost!"
61 Augury
63 Little guy
64 Tough
65 Disaffect
67 Crested coats
68 Proud ladies?
69 Grade-school trio
72 Exodus crossing
73 Ho's hi's
74 Drumbeater
76 Deal with sin
77 Gloss
78 Fifth Avenue store
79 "Socrate" composer Satie
83 White blanket
84 John Wooden Center school
85 Get gooey
88 Chain letters?

26 MUSICAL SHORTCUTS by Roger H. Courtney
28 Across is the official state song of Louisiana.

ACROSS

1 O'Neal in "The Technical Writer"
6 Pistol pop
10 Alter the script
14 Leave hastily
19 Nimble
20 River to Kassel
21 City near Lake Tahoe
22 Child's transport
23 Rock bottom
24 Anderson in "Too Good to Be True"
25 Novelist Sillitoe
26 Pointed
27 Cyclist LeMond
28 Jimmie Davis/Charles Mitchell song
31 "Siddhartha" author
33 Original Muse of song
34 Viacom ___
35 Flivvers
38 Slip away from
39 Genuflected
43 Brother of Linus and Lucy
44 Failures
45 Anti-DUI org.
46 Lonely number
47 "Yesterday!"
48 Frank Loesser song
52 Sra., formerly
53 Disinfectant's target
54 Days in a novena
55 Agatha's contemporary
56 Underground worker
57 "Don't move!"
59 Like a chain of hills
62 They're beyond help
63 Erudition
64 Half a Gauguin book
65 Painter Chagall
66 Light a match
69 PUZZLE THEME
72 Regards highly
76 Like arugula
77 Overseas mil. addresses
78 IRS functionaries
80 ___-Ude, Russia
81 Francis or Frank
82 Carrie Jacobs Bond song
85 "Sideways" subject
86 Identify
87 Father of Balder
88 It takes a verb
89 New ___ on life
90 Made tea
92 King of Troy
94 Two fins
95 Bovine's playground
96 Breakfast dish
97 Dracula, for one
99 John Barry/Leslie Bricusse song
102 Second apple biter
106 Quebec peninsula
108 Caribbean music
109 Once, at one time
110 On guard
111 "Clean your room!", e.g.
112 Robbie Knievel's dad
113 Political contest
114 "Amores" language
115 Wampum units
116 Cincy team
117 Catch sight of
118 ___ large (generally)

DOWN

1 Space drink
2 Gravy thickener
3 It rises and falls
4 Joe Brooks song
5 Boulogne-sur-___
6 Bartók and Lugosi
7 Venerate
8 Hawaii's state bird
9 Monaco's ruling family
10 Deleted data
11 Humbug
12 Empty-headed
13 Whale weights
14 Buckley's "___ Glass"
15 "Purple Rain" performer
16 Gimlet garnish
17 "Runaway Bride" hero
18 Spread alfalfa
28 ___ Arizona Memorial
29 Brooklynese pronoun
30 Pilgrim at Ajodhya
32 Tennyson's twilight
35 Rugged rocks
36 Adjust a clock
37 Brazil macaw
38 Father of calculus
39 Welles citizen
40 Ben on "Bonanza"
41 Computer command
42 Darlings
44 Bear lair
45 Weather forecast
48 Harden
49 Fisherman's desire
50 Woody Harrelson, for one
51 Prior to
52 Oscar-winning Max Steiner film score
56 Humorist Sahl
58 Turtlelike
60 Unavailable
61 June bug
62 Starlike?
65 English tea?
66 Reacts to an insult
67 Dogma
68 Coloratura's asset
69 Atop
70 "Mazel ___!"
71 Rugby formation
73 Cuban boy in the 2000 news
74 Pastor's home
75 Vile smile
77 "Put ___ on it!"
79 Groan getter
82 Paradigm
83 Coalesce
84 Wedding gifts
87 They'll flip your lid
89 Golfer Mattiace
91 Married quietly
92 Ticketed
93 Competitors
94 Pre-Wed. date
96 Golf wear
97 Pancho's pal
98 String ensemble
99 Org. concerned with BSE
100 Flanders river
101 Sandwich type
103 Brent Spiner role
104 Similar (to)
105 Darn right?
106 Jack-tar
107 "___ we there yet?"
110 Pastor's robe

LADIES FIRST   by Sam Bellotto Jr.
The first lady at 23 Across was nicknamed the "Secret President."

ACROSS

1 "Rosamond" composer
5 Underwater ray
10 Encounter
15 Orderly
19 Blues legend Redbone
20 Part of 22 Across
21 "Take me ___ the ballgame . . ."
22 Stevedore's org.
23 Mrs. Woodrow Wilson
26 When two hands meet
27 View from Jiddah
28 Windsor Castle neighbor
29 Legal residence
31 Quoits target
32 Albanian river
35 Stats at Shea
37 Oft-broken promise
38 Mrs. Zachary Taylor
46 Goddess of Hades: Var.
47 "Mastodonia" author Clifford D.
48 Gym ball
49 Disseminated
52 Broken
55 Me, to Mitterrand
56 Loess and loam
57 Ocular layer
58 Mrs. James Madison
62 Prefix for content
63 "Dr. Vegas" star
64 Short-story awards
65 Dadaist sculptor
66 Curmudgeon
69 Cuts corners, in a sense
75 Seagoing raptor
76 Anthropoids
78 Roundup target
79 Stop–dime links
80 Mrs. Dwight D. Eisenhower
85 Slothful
86 NYC's Stage and Carnegie
87 Key near Ctrl
88 Like ___ of bricks
89 They disappeared in 1681
90 Chad of baseball
91 Hosp. ward
93 Birdman of Alcatraz
96 Mrs. John F. Kennedy
102 ET's craft
103 Burgess' top "droog"
104 Suffix for leather
105 "Superman" baddie Luthor
107 "Shark Tale" has one
112 Some winged queens
114 Action-freezing light
116 Dart
117 Mrs. John Tyler
121 "___ fan tutte": Mozart
122 Draw forth
123 Identified
124 End of Missouri's motto
125 Job particular, briefly
126 Remove a lawn
127 Hidden treasure
128 Watched

DOWN

1 Advisory
2 Cash in
3 "I haven't a clue"
4 "The Two Towers" trees
5 Sadat's successor
6 A year in Dali's life
7 Nothing
8 Painted metalware
9 Two, in the tabs
10 Good brandies
11 Kind of a nut
12 Just ___ (not much)
13 Town on the Vire
14 Bedtime drink
15 Fools
16 Aristocratic Wells race
17 MP's concern
18 Ditty
24 Bet both ways
25 "Key Largo" heroine
30 Psychic parts
33 "Best Boy" director Wohl
34 Vexed
36 Schusser's wear
39 Perlman in "Matilda"
40 Freshwater duck
41 Island NE of Hong Kong
42 Rested
43 Crocus, for one
44 Recounted
45 Pinafore letters
49 Japanese sport
50 Spoon-shaped
51 Use a torch
53 Foster mother of Oedipus
54 Peacock feather feature
56 Ma's cello is one
58 College in Lincoln, Nebraska
59 Hold
60 Volkswagen model
61 Facilitated
63 Count Ipanov in "Fedora"
67 Like the frog
68 He won a Grammy for "Smooth"
70 "___ There": Simple Plan hit
71 Little, to Lautrec
72 Bufonid
73 Car designer Ferrari
74 Writes the checks
77 Tanguay or Gabor
80 Prefix for bucks
81 Tess Durbeyfield's victim
82 Scottish Celt
83 Pre-coll.
84 Medicate
85 New Jersey city
86 Ashcroft's former org.
89 Down-filled quilts
91 Fixed a squeak again
92 Tardy
94 Falderal
95 Reason for a ball call
97 Educators' org.
98 Director Riefenstahl
99 Alive
100 Kay Thompson girl
101 Buying incentive
106 Inert gas
107 Army E-3's
108 Unappetizing dish
109 Diva Stevens
110 Campbell in "Scream 3"
111 Pontiac sports cars
113 Sore reminder?
115 AAA suggestions
118 Half a Jockamo Crawford title
119 Health plan
120 Gun the engine

28 FOODIES by Elizabeth C. Gorski

The muscle cars at 121 Down were previously manufactured from 1964–74.

ACROSS

1 Butler's love
6 Short-legged, long-haired dog
14 "I know, however . . ."
20 Cancels
21 Patched a jacket?
22 Recorded
23 Foodie who likes finger food?
25 Kampala's country
26 Clam or buck
27 Tweety ___
28 Axillary
30 Hupmobile rivals
31 Beer ingredient
33 Nipper's corp.
36 Heads-up
38 Hoarse laugh
42 Oriole Sammy
44 Kick upstairs
46 Harris and Wynn
49 Gets some airtime?
51 Epicurean foodie with a burning desire?
54 Permeate
55 Rodeo rope
56 Most favorable conditions
57 Antibody regulator
58 Costa ___
60 "CHiPs" star Estrada
63 Hogwash
64 Green-lights
66 Frasier's TV brother
69 Make better
71 "Sorta" suffix
72 Foodie who's gaga over guacamole?
76 Center of Centre Court
78 Picture, slangily
79 "The ___ Anxiety": Bernstein
80 Hip-hop Dr.
81 Melville novel
83 Riven
85 Stone and Stallone
87 Prepare to bask in the sun
91 Missouri Compromise president
93 Muse of poetry
96 Sidewalk festival, perhaps
98 Foodie who has no beef with beef?
101 Providing with authority
102 Eur. country
103 One who spread the Word
104 Queens stadium
106 Ladies of Spain, for short
107 Rhone River city
108 Barn bird
110 "Das Lied von der ___": Mahler
112 Marseille "mine"
115 "___ soup yet?"
117 Prefix meaning "outer"
119 Mutilate
124 Country cottage fabric
126 Foodie who likes fluff pieces?
130 Play with no intermission
131 Double-crossers
132 On-line calculator, say
133 Spherical bacterium
134 Achilles' heel
135 Impudent

DOWN

1 How LPs are re-issued
2 Sunshine cracker
3 Hughes jump
4 Dance music
5 State in NE India
6 "Great Expectations" hero
7 Explodes, as a volcano
8 Annan of the United Nations
9 Deduce
10 Beak
11 Brown URL suffix
12 Couch potato's station
13 Kindle desire: Var.
14 "Thanks so much!"
15 Chang's twin
16 Commencement
17 Bugaboo
18 Bride's hairstyle
19 Twinings selection
24 Cleared the slate
29 Like a bump on ___
32 Luckless one
34 Tax experts
35 Magazine pieces?
37 Do another hitch
38 Absorbed
39 Pierre's "with"
40 Mule's jackass, e.g.
41 His work went to the dogs?
43 Workers' org. formed in 1955
45 Slender reed
46 Couturier Pucci
47 Populace
48 Impetigo cause
50 "The ___ the Town" (1942)
52 Tiny Teletubby
53 ACLU concerns
59 Rep. that includes Java
61 Regard as concrete
62 Chapel vow
65 Acted offensively?
67 Alphabetic trio
68 Afternoon break
70 Cards with cups
72 Sorry sort
73 Munched brunch
74 Copyediting marks
75 Rousseau and Jefferson, e.g.
76 "Contains ___" (food-label claim)
77 Overdo it on stage
82 ___ pro nobis
84 Bivouac shelter
86 Christmas Club member
88 Animal house
89 Bone by the radius
90 Violin tuners
92 "It's a deal!"
94 Move, in realtor lingo
95 Not very many
97 Instructive computer file
99 Free electrons
100 Backs up
105 Prefix meaning "different"
107 Lavender
109 Turns on the highway
111 Roof projections
112 Book of Rev.
113 Like Presley's early records
114 Cartel acronym
116 Madrid Stock Exchange optimist?
118 Hoof sound
120 "That's ___ bad idea"
121 Pontiac muscle cars
122 Late July babies
123 Congerlike
125 "ER" venue
127 Former Mideast org.
128 "Tsk, tsk!"
129 "Spring ahead" letters

MIXED DOUBLES   by Fred Piscop
"Double, double toil and trouble . . ."

ACROSS

1 Mr. Peanut's anklewear
6 Blind piece
10 Banded stone
15 Times to call, in ads
19 Hearing-related
20 Eight minutes per mile, say
21 "Cheaper by the ___" (1950)
22 List heading
23 "Goosebumps" author
24 Far from arable
25 Computer match service?
27 Garden-variety nerd?
30 All, for one
31 MS. markers
32 Drags to court
34 Big name in banking
35 Makes greater
40 Come face-to-face
42 Most collectible, maybe
46 "Uh-uh!"
47 Tear carriers
49 Second section
52 Classroom nickname
53 ". . . ___ quit!"
54 Eta's follower
56 St. ___, Switzerland
58 Moo goo ___ pan
59 Lawyer Kuby
60 Ken Jennings' $2,520,700, e.g.?
62 Some diner orders
63 Caine title role
65 Place to build
66 Seuss turtle
68 Lamenters, perhaps
71 Postgame segment
74 Be postponed
77 Quick-witted
79 Sale-tag caveat
81 Quick-witted
82 Bandleader Puente
84 Bib?
89 Use a snifter
90 ___ Mazen (Abbas)
91 Trial balloon
92 Cub Scout leader
93 Bump off
94 ___ diem
96 Struck out
98 Crystal-gazers
100 Idiot-light word
101 Dog trainer's supply
103 Just-for-fun activity
105 "___ a Dance": Rodgers & Hart
107 Physicist Bohr
110 One can't do one
112 Buddy List® co.
113 Best boy, e.g.
117 Cause of an oil leak?
123 Reaganisms?
125 Maul or awl
126 Pottery maker, at times
127 Out of control
128 ___ HOOKS (crate legend)
129 Egg cell
130 Ouzo flavoring
131 In a blue funk
132 Job extras
133 Brings home
134 In a pet

DOWN

1 Smart talk
2 Tee off, in miniature golf
3 Song from "Turandot"
4 Leather worker
5 Went downhill fast
6 Go a round
7 Fat in the can
8 Tummy upsetters
9 Night watchman's problem, perhaps
10 Toss in
11 Stick with a prod
12 Quetzalcoatl worshiper
13 An elephant has four
14 Win over
15 Bric-a-brac holder
16 Field mouse
17 Fall site
18 Word processing function
26 Like chicory, vis-à-vis coffee
28 Discerning
29 Hatchery sound
33 Sordid
35 Arctic jacket
36 King of pop
37 Cleft, at times?
38 It may go off the wall
39 48 Down parts
41 Pull a sulky, perhaps
43 Mouse-catching requirement?
44 "Amscray!"
45 "___ means war!"
48 Way up or down
50 Stackable item
51 Theodore in "The Enemy Below"
55 Galería display
57 Hatcher of "Desperate Housewives"
60 Give a razzing to
61 Window sticker
62 Online journal
64 ___-European languages
67 Deck material
69 Took a hack
70 Begot
72 On the briny
73 They're drafted
75 Draw out
76 Drives away
78 Bit of mosaic
80 Quire member
82 What good hosts have
83 Girder type
85 Ring sound
86 Diner freebie
87 General Robt. ___
88 Of the body
91 Fixation
95 Far from cool
97 Beat the tar out of
99 Pooh-pooh
102 Makes ready
104 "Annie Hall" Oscar winner
106 May in "Small Time Crooks"
108 Fall off the wagon
109 Look from Snidely
111 Valuable find
113 17 Down figure
114 Clash of heavyweights
115 "No more!"
116 Panzer
118 Whale the tar out of
119 Spreading trees
120 "Trinity" author
121 "___ we forget . . ."
122 Deuce topper
124 Joe Louis had 54

SOUND EFFECTS   by Nancy Nicholson Joline
126 Across wins the Groaner Award for the most outrageous pun.

ACROSS

1 "Blazing Saddles" sheriff
5 Periods
9 Muslim religious leader
13 Scrooge visitor
19 ___-cat
20 Music award category
21 Zilch
22 Strasbourg's locale
23 So-so singing group?
25 Darling star follower?
27 Single-masted vessel
28 Hedren in "The Birds"
30 Slapstick missile
31 Take care of
32 Postulations
34 Take the lead
35 Gypsy's calling card?
37 Brief moment
39 Like many letters to the editor
41 Iris rings
46 "Darn!"
50 Put up
52 Christo, e.g.?
54 ___ Rios, Jamaica
55 Evaporated milk brand
56 U.K. record label
58 Freshly painted
59 "Very funny!"
60 What a picky restaurant critic does?
64 Poker player, at times
66 Neighborhood pub
67 Zetterling in "The Witches"
68 ___ Khan
69 Most unusual
70 Didn't hit
73 Certain questions
76 Flower part
80 "Wow!"
82 Auction ending
83 Grind
88 Rudolf Nureyev and Marat Safin, e.g.
89 Insurrection on the camping trail?
92 Theater sign
93 "The 4400" network
95 Ending with Ecuador
96 Quentin's "Kill Bill" star
97 Memento
98 ___ Terrible orchestra member?
101 Endangered hoofed mammal
103 Some other time
104 Portuguese resort
105 Fab Four name
107 Adage
109 Portray on stage
111 Bodybuilder's pride
113 Midwest capital
118 Midwestern Indians
122 Contemporary art?
123 Crops crops
125 Swain
126 Head music?
129 Recondite roaster?
131 Subordinate
132 Dash
133 About
134 Singer James
135 Alternatives to vans
136 "Darn!"
137 Near East gulf
138 Show disrespect

DOWN

1 Lift
2 Place for a bracelet
3 Spy mission
4 Chevy truck
5 Part of RSA
6 Bearded one
7 New York Harbor island
8 Questioning one
9 Rajiv Gandhi's mother
10 Fannie ___
11 Screenwriter, often
12 "West Side Story" role
13 Was in session
14 ___ of Paris
15 Man, e.g.
16 Libertine
17 "Law & Order: SVU" star
18 Indy driver Palmroth
24 Elects
26 Sonora shawl
29 Like a fool and his money
33 Oozes slowly
36 House delivery?
38 Candy-store group
40 Stab
42 Significant ___
43 Hansen of NPR
44 Phoenix origin
45 Institute
46 Funny person
47 Nymph who loved Narcissus
48 Smart
49 Hawaiian coffee
51 Lab burners
53 Babies often elicit these
57 Hamm of soccer
61 Fudd in "Slick Hare"
62 Luna in "Frida"
63 Stand for Seurat
65 Old-hat
71 Pancreas product
72 Setting for "The English Patient"
74 Scheme
75 One of a Dumas trio
76 U.S. Open winner Jones
77 Urban honkers
78 Half-cocked
79 Christ of the Andes sculptor Alonso
81 Basque separatist org.
84 Glen Gray's Casa ___ Orchestra
85 Mary Kay competitor
86 Beach of Florida
87 The Old Sod
89 "That ain't ___"
90 It's beside the sides
91 Gold standard?
94 Islamic greeting
99 "The Music Man" star
100 "Great Expectations" girl
102 Santa Anita Park site
106 Airport areas
108 Alan ___ Arkin
110 Jon of "Two and a Half Men"
112 Support the economy
114 Reads intently
115 "You Must Love Me" musical
116 "Endymion" poet
117 Hiding place for Polonius
118 Doctrines
119 Thirties migrant
120 It may be in knots
121 Capital of Samoa
124 Parched
127 Cricket sides
128 Straw grass
130 Female swan

31 BALL TEAM by Michael Collins
81 Across was the hero of a 2005 sci-fi digitally animated film.

ACROSS

1 "Round and Round" singer
5 Cuba ___ (rum drink)
10 Standee's handful
15 Moistens, in a way
19 Closely related
20 Henry Ford's son
21 Dieter's temptation
22 "Dream Children" essayist
23 Actress on the ball team?
25 Novelist on the ball team?
27 Graffiti or litter
28 ". . . ___ and a haircut, two bits"
30 Seat of County Kerry
31 Spanish pianist José
34 Bonanza find
35 Country renamed in 1939
36 1951 Oscar winner Karl
39 IV part
41 Raised
45 "___ Gold" (Peter Fonda film)
46 Reynolds merger partner
47 Veil fabric
48 Zoo swinger
49 Try for a part
50 Forced labor camp
51 Go like a crab
52 "Vissi d'___": Puccini
53 Sheet-music abbr.
54 Plant, so to speak
55 Penny-pinching
57 Hand out
58 Seaside resort near L.A.
61 Chip in
62 Dahl in "Slightly Scarlet"
63 Joule parts
64 Thumbs-down giver
66 Student's acquisition, maybe
67 Author Huxley
69 Hammer-on-the-fing ernail reaction
70 Racing form
74 "Borstal Boy" author
75 In the arms of Morpheus
77 Days of old
78 Coverage co.
79 Strawberry ___
80 Put in place
81 Rodney Copperbottom, for one
83 Pesky sort
84 Pundit Coulter
85 Fuzzbuster detection
86 Soda purchase
87 Socialite Mesta
88 Middle-Aged?
90 Madonna portrayal
91 Checked for ID
92 People of Burma
93 Mahmoud Abbas' gp.
94 Cloverleaf part
96 Key's inspiration, for short
99 Danish dough?
101 How some sci-fi aliens come
105 Singer on the ball team?
107 Actress on the ball team?
110 Suit material?
111 Elle in "Legally Blonde"
112 ". . . better man than I am, ___ Din!": Kipling
113 Designer letters
114 Is in the hole
115 Swerved off course
116 Ken ___ Kesey
117 New York diamond

DOWN

1 It may be tiered
2 Not bad
3 Place to get stuck
4 Like a Möbius strip
5 French president (1932–40)
6 Ne'er-do-well
7 Tenderfoot's org.
8 Camcorder button
9 Lodge fellows
10 Much of North Africa
11 Valuable find
12 T. ___ Price (investment firm)
13 Soul singer Shola
14 Muon or pion
15 Sling mud at
16 Mideast carrier
17 Like Nestor
18 Fill beyond full
24 They're on staffs
26 Disney's Ludwig Von ___
29 Joyous dance
32 Actor on the ball team?
33 Machu Picchu builder
35 Foray
36 Bit of cave art
37 Last Oldsmobile ever made
38 Jurist on the ball team?
40 Glad rags
41 Wild West figure on the ball team?
42 Tennis player on the ball team?
43 Writer Sinclair
44 Calvin of the PGA
46 Subtle glow
47 Like sunglasses
50 Take a shot
51 Deadly septet
52 Hajji's deity
54 Compressed-air weapon
56 Hose shade
57 Cropped up
59 Pun reaction
60 Ward ___ (local politico)
62 Argus-eyed
65 Took a powder
67 James ___ Garfield
68 Sierra ___
71 Not as good as 2 Down
72 Meyer in "Paths of Glory"
73 In great shape
75 Quinn of "Benny & Joon"
76 ___-dieu (prayer bench)
80 Brutality
82 Snorkel's pooch
83 Considers carefully
85 Where to dry out
86 Columbia gridder
87 Gaucho's milieu
89 Archipelago units
90 Under the table
91 Moulin Rouge dance
93 Novel or essay
95 Fab Four name
96 Engaged in
97 Winning ticket for a losing horse, perhaps
98 Links warning
99 Had down cold
100 Sphere's lack
102 Woodstock cross
103 Gelato holder
104 "Orinoco Flow" singer
106 Where chanteys are sung
108 Ingrid's "Anastasia" costar
109 Tiny colonist

ACROSS

1 Stadium stratum
5 Loud sound or loudly sound
10 Rosa of opera
15 City scourge
19 Timber tool
20 They're long on luxury?
21 Seventh UN secretary-general
22 Model Banks
23 Nicholson/Gaynor twin bill
26 "Yoicks!"
27 Marconi-rigged vessels
28 Herring nets
29 Chase work
31 It can be wild
33 Tots up
34 Stuff
35 Eastwood/Stamp twin bill
41 Shoelace thingie
42 Antique auto
43 Broadway auntie
44 Not nay
45 'Twixt Mich. and Minn.
46 New Zealand soldier
49 Oldsters' org.
52 Dortmund denial
54 Play where "robot" arose
57 Heston/Depardieu twin bill
62 Shopaholic's favorite word?
63 Love to pieces
64 Far-sighted one?
65 Made a ring adjustment
67 Grow together
70 Maverick
71 Like Polyphemus
72 Gathers, as support
73 Let loose like Leo
74 Bubble gum giant
75 Yours and mine
76 De Niro/Costner twin bill
82 Poivre's partner
83 Belknap of "Medical Investigation"
84 Literary governess
85 Bluish purple
86 Designer Saint Laurent
88 It's in central Louisiana
91 Every go-with
94 Grasp the joke
95 Observant one
97 Keach/Crystal twin bill
102 Causing wear
104 Denver tower
105 Knowing the latest
106 Exaggerated number
107 Gets more out of
110 Joined together, as resources
114 Roman raiment
115 Shields/O'Neal twin bill
118 Month after Av
119 Pine product
120 "Less Than Zero" novelist
121 1973 Musante series
122 Box score column
123 Mandalay Bay machines
124 Egyptian Peace Prize Nobelist
125 Laurel in "Hollywood Party"

DOWN

1 Touches base
2 TV's "American ___"
3 Bass Pinza
4 Eminence
5 Flower (with or without the esses)
6 Lucy in "Kill Bill"
7 Totals: Abbr.
8 Architect Mies van der ___
9 Sighting
10 Flew, as time
11 Not a triviality
12 Written with one flat
13 Did like Drake
14 Imbiber's bender
15 Short memo takers?
16 Culkin/Rooney twin bill
17 Fruit with rind but no rhyme
18 Thingamajig
24 Risky venture
25 Mayberry sheriff Taylor
30 All over
32 Letters that go in an empty slot
35 Victoria's Secret offerings
36 "Johnny ___" (1966)
37 Like hot-fudge syrup
38 Spin doctor's concern
39 King of tragedy
40 Andrews in 36 Down
45 Improved a road
47 Some have snooze buttons
48 Formally forks over
50 Preplanned Virginia city
51 Fellow folks
53 "Misty" composer Garner
55 1997 Peter Fonda role
56 Salmon-spawning area
58 Street sign
59 Rock-boring tool
60 Close
61 Caterwaul
62 ___ Nevada range
66 No-___ (gnat)
67 Kerfuffles
68 Rock's Mötley ___
69 Temple/Cruise twin bill
70 Hindu address
74 Some circus performers
77 Earth goddess
78 Manhattan Project scientist
79 Prodigious
80 Assert affirmatively
81 New York nine
83 Eagle abode
87 Virgins
89 Like some nights
90 Blocks out
92 Gulager in "Skyward"
93 Most with it
95 Spay
96 Faux gold
97 Seasoning seed
98 Recovery rms.
99 Is on the mound
100 Whispers sweet nothings
101 ___ Berry Farm
103 Changes direction
108 She knew scat's where it's at
109 "I'll take it!"
111 Filthy lucre
112 Humorist Bombeck
113 Cannon in "Caddyshack II"
116 Award for a Brit. officer
117 By way of

33 DOUBLE FEATURE–PART II   by Joel Kaplow
The second of a twin bill.

ACROSS

1 Dances with dips
7 Different ones
13 David's third son
20 Gives a heads-up
21 Civil War battle site
22 Fearsome funnel
23 Cage/Gibson twin bill
25 Re three
26 Emilio's egg
27 High flat
28 Alaska Highway, once
30 "Indubitably!"
31 Spanish spousal unit
33 "Gentlemen Prefer Blondes" heroine
36 Hilton-Jacobs/Cooper twin bill
42 A half pint has eight
45 Sacristy hanging
46 ___ Vegas Bowl
47 Holiday for ham
49 The cat's meow
50 Come back again
53 Kind of queen
54 Unsavory cracker?
56 "Playboy" columnist Baber
57 Cusack/Dreyfuss twin bill
61 Reacted to rancor
63 Tactic type
64 Eterne
65 Where many couples have met
67 700-mile-long African river
68 Snowball fighters, e.g.
71 Show shame
73 Theater section
76 Salvation and Arnie's
78 Danny Thomas interjection
79 Simply supple
83 Put to use
85 Williams/Hepburn twin bill
88 Muslim cap
89 See 84 Down
91 Quite an accomplishment
92 Ketchup origin
93 Expunge
95 Hedy in "Samson and Delilah"
97 E-9, for one
99 Bon mot
100 New Hampshire statesman John
102 Streisand/Presley twin bill
106 Honorary title
108 It's spotted in Mexico
109 Before card or ball
111 He had an act with Rudman
113 Places of refuge
114 George of "Just Shoot Me"
118 Evergreen State capital
121 Peck/Beatty twin bill
124 Round Table knight
125 Toyota sedan
126 More unnerving
127 It gets by a gasket
128 Change the picture
129 Oscar winner Jackson

DOWN

1 Dash dial
2 Baseball's Moises
3 NBA's Hilario
4 Driveway filler
5 Lazy
6 Latvia, prev.
7 Membrane permeation
8 1980 Jamie Lee Curtis film
9 "Sugar Lips" trumpeter
10 Marienthal in "Tucker"
11 Cape near Lisbon
12 Green onion
13 Petal perfume
14 Third-largest island
15 Mr., in Madras
16 "SNL" alumna Gasteyer
17 Sutherland/Romano twin bill
18 Jon Arbuckle's dog
19 Soft shoes
24 "Hi, haole!"
29 Island in Brooklyn
32 Tower of power
34 Mario's game brother
35 Cessation
36 Complaining fish?
37 Oil: Rx
38 Past plump
39 Towel word in Dogpatch
40 Watts in "I Heart Huckabees"
41 "The Sixth Sense" star
43 Stand for something
44 "Tribute" playwright
48 Fixed wickerwork
51 Campus church
52 Provide a position
53 Philip of "Great Expectations"
55 Cranky canine's comment
58 "Come off it!"
59 Rain hard
60 Zero
62 Laundry-saving practice
66 La ___ Tar Pits
69 Slothful
70 West Indies coral
72 Admiral Zumwalt
73 Guitar predecessors
74 Hokkaido port city
75 Moore/Welles twin bill
77 Stem counterpart
80 "The Sound of Music" family
81 Put the bite on
82 Flat wood?
84 "The Beverly Hillbillies" star (with 89-A)
86 Grant in "Mr. Lucky"
87 Bikini, for one
90 1994 trade pact
94 Some homophone
96 Libya's Khadafy
97 Pilfering, in Plymouth
98 Grow louder, to Liszt: Abbr.
101 Arm-twisting
103 Folk legend Lightfoot
104 Inhospitable-sounding inn?
105 Pied-___
107 Severely sore
109 Spacely Sprockets competitor Cogswell ___
110 Fonda's Oscar-nominated role
112 "Get the lead out!"
113 Jean Auel heroine
115 Pain result?
116 Got a hole in one
117 Vega's constellation
119 Rand McNally product
120 Entertaining Zadora
122 Humbug go-with
123 St. Bernard's burden

ACROSS

1 Dearth
5 Summarize
10 Near by
15 Egyptian fertility goddess
19 Take care of a pressing detail
20 Love, in Lyon
21 Luann's love
22 Greek walkway
23 Chinese: Comb. form
24 Ms. Rogers' siestas?
26 Trilled
27 Flavored lozenge
29 Junta
30 Curriculum element
32 Former British Airways jet
33 Author Rita ___ Brown
34 Egyptian peninsula
35 Carryalls
36 Field spaniel color
38 Constrict
39 Ominous
42 Afresh
44 Nicotine ___
45 Drug agents
46 ___ Dawn Chong
47 Drudge
48 Minuet-like dance
49 Home-schooled student
50 Vonnegut or Russell
51 Half-score
52 Sophia in "Soleil"
53 Hazarded
54 Twin crystal
55 Bawls out
57 Handel opera
58 Thurman Munson was one
59 Liabilities seem likely?
63 Bernadette in "The Jerk"
66 Mideast liquors
67 Tag a second time
71 Spills (over)
72 Clutches
73 Lacy mat
75 Ruckus
76 Qualifying race

77 Bleachers
78 Like a gnu
79 Therefore
80 In addition
81 Sapor
82 More calamitous
83 "___ in Toyland"
84 Complete failures
86 Some sculptures
87 "Detroit City" singer
88 Uptight
89 Shreds or rends
90 Ailing
91 Food-label abbr.
94 "Sic transit ___ mundi"
96 Believer in Dharma
97 Spectrosco-py, e.g.
99 Boudoir
100 Tom's deficiencies?
103 Ohms' repricrals
104 Proficient
105 Outlandish
106 Flightless bird
107 Navajo ___ Talkers
108 Lichen
109 Measly
110 Feats of derring-do
111 Parrots

DOWN

1 Speech problems
2 Renée Fleming solos
3 Inmate's transports?
4 Granny or square
5 One-piece sleeve
6 Hirsch in "The Emperor's Club"
7 Cornet
8 Summer mo.
9 Zone
10 Algiers quarter
11 Veranda
12 Phonic
13 Drench

14 Settle comfortably
15 Magazine numbers
16 Headliner's pickup?
17 Charged atoms
18 Guru, e.g.
25 Horse farm
28 She married David Bowie
31 Porter's regretful miss
34 Suppress
35 Fatigued
37 Black gold
38 Macadamize
39 Glossy fabric
40 "Harlem Nocturne" composer Hagen
41 Prop a golf ball again
42 "___ girl!"
43 Attends
44 Indian Zoroastrian
45 Hospital employee
48 Plays 18
49 Pool covers

50 Roo's mother
52 Waiters in ambush
53 Study pieces
54 Masculine
56 Adroit
57 Uses a dirk
58 Relinquish
60 Tiffany weights
61 Riled up
62 More parched
63 "Nonsense!"
64 "___ and Her Men" (Ingrid Bergman film)
65 Amphibian's implements?
68 Haircutter's skip?
69 Rim
70 "Gentlemen Prefer Blondes" author
72 "The Last Remake of Beau ___" (1977)
73 "501" game
74 Till bills

77 Chorizo and saveloy
78 Judged wrongly
79 Corn spike
81 Collette in "The Hours"
82 Couples
83 Cotillion
85 Messenger of myth
86 Elizabeth of "Pride and Prejudice"
87 Explosions
89 Link up
90 Signed a pact
92 Device with two electrodes
93 Self-important ones
94 15.4321 grains
95 Gray wolf
96 Zeus' spouse
97 Tract division
98 Village People hit
101 Kind of room or hall
102 Lifetime

35 SAW ABOUT SPEAKING   by Harvey Estes
Perhaps we should add "Monty or . . ." to the clue at 119 Across.

ACROSS

1 ER priority system
7 Worn sheets?
12 Suite spot
16 Fallen space station
19 "Lost Horizon" author
20 Pass into law
21 Comply with
23 **Saw about speaking: Part 1**
25 Suggested
26 Fab Four member
27 Put up with
28 Noted Joseph Wiseman role
29 Pfefferberg in "Schindler's List"
30 Fab Four dos
32 Columnist Hopper
34 Saying nothing
35 Mom and pop, e.g.
39 **Saw: Part 2**
42 Busy
43 One who hits the tennis ball back and forth?
44 Nullify
45 Salt, chemically
46 Open wide
48 What history often repeats
51 Penn., for one
54 **Saw: Part 3**
58 Painter Bonheur
59 Songwriter Bacharach
60 "Get Off of My Cloud" group
61 DePaul mascot, in blue
63 Barbershop figure
64 Stop-sign shape
66 **Saw: Part 4**
67 Pacific group
69 City on the Loire
70 Have coming
71 Queen's name
72 Part of IMHO
73 Nepal locale
75 **Saw: Part 5**
79 U-turn from NNW
80 Teeming
82 The bulk
83 Pinup Hayworth
84 Uncredited role in "The Thin Man"
85 "Delta of Venus" author Nin
88 Broker, at times
90 **End of saw**
95 Jumping-off place
96 "Camelot" composer
97 Up to the time of
98 "Shane" actor
99 Morales in "Paid in Full"
100 "Law & Order: SVU" star
102 Used one's scull?
104 "She ___": Jay & the Americans
109 The A380, for one
111 **Monastic oath based on this saw?**
113 Fetches
114 Thumb-turning critic
115 "Man of La ___"
116 Go for it
117 Eureka hook-on
118 Lightheaded
119 Dragon slain by Apollo

DOWN

1 What have we here
2 Falling-out
3 "Superman" producer Salkind
4 Suffix with fabric
5 Haute-cuisine patron
6 Ref. work
7 Revival shelters
8 Savvy about
9 Alternative fuel
10 Campus community
11 Dorm room, sometimes
12 Gung-ho
13 Aesir bigwig
14 "Curses!"
15 "The" place for opera
16 Noble Italian family name
17 Leaning letter
18 Take turns
22 Send back
24 Cold-blooded killers
28 Banned pesticide
31 Pizza herb
33 '50s sitcom name
34 "Weekend's almost here!"
35 "Five Women" author Jaffe
36 Spirited horse
37 Dressed for a part
38 Healthful
39 Like unheard children, proverbially
40 Lithographer of Americana
41 Vincent Lopez theme
43 Hot places to chill out
47 "I'll say!"
49 Disney sci-fi flick
50 Ham, to Noah
51 "Keep Your ___ Up"
52 "Star Trek: TNG" counselor
53 Razor name
55 Glad rags
56 Nose-wrinkling stimulus
57 Fork over
59 Grizzly catcher
62 SAT section
63 Hermione Granger, for one
64 Soul singer Redding
65 Bad points
66 Deterioration
67 88, for one
68 Stopped bleeding
70 "The Princess Diaries" princess
71 Son in Genesis 4:26
73 Bubbly wine
74 Odette, by day
76 Jannings of old films
77 Villanova's football conf.
78 "The Longest ___" (2005)
80 Queens stadium name
81 Heisman winner Leinart
84 As you please
86 Ernie Kovacs trio
87 Permitted
89 Colorful Virginia soil
90 BoSox div.
91 More prying
92 Every 525,600 minutes
93 "C'est la ___!"
94 Small colonist
95 Some diaper changers
98 Grove of Cooperstown
100 The goods
101 Co. leaders
103 Logophile's love
105 Flat fee?
106 Barely move
107 Cave effect
108 Official with a list
110 Bull tail
111 Relax (with "out")
112 Little rascal

FARM CLUB   by Jay Sullivan
The irony of 37 Down is that his name actually does mean "cat."

ACROSS

1 Work shift
5 Violin-family members
10 Fish hooks
15 Beach blanket
19 On the safe side
20 "Here we are as in ___ days . . ."
21 Throw for ___
22 Nevermore?
23 Pastoral symphony?
25 Fearsome bark?
27 30's recovery program
28 SE Asian mountain people
30 Itty-bitty
31 Family men
32 Take care
34 Max. or min.
35 Strong suit
38 They change hands at the track
39 Dialogue
44 Went a-courtin'?
45 "Our Man Flint" star
46 Large accounts
47 Birthplace of The Boss
48 Lennon's relict
49 What the black sheep had?
51 Close ones
52 City on the Tyne
54 Nonchalance
55 Prickly pears
56 What's left
57 Winter weather wear
59 Werner in "Ship of Fools"
60 Stick around
61 Olympic Motto start
63 Cash on hand?
64 Serengeti laugher
66 Quire members
67 French encyclopedist
70 Have a home-cooked meal
71 Pessimist's word
72 Spurs' old home
74 Defeat at rasslin'
75 Ibsen turkey?
78 "Wheel of Fortune" request
79 It's quite a stretch
80 "John Brown's Body" author
81 Like linoleum
82 Bickering
83 Malamute munchies
85 News media
86 Simpson and Kudrow
87 Cleopatra's killer
88 Diploma distinction
89 Not 'neath
90 "Some Like It Hot" star
93 Long-time Chicago maestro
94 Campus life
98 Rooster's wake-up call?
100 Long-faced horse?
103 Son of Jacob
104 "Amerika" novelist
105 High-toned fellow
106 Hatcher of "Desperate Housewives"
107 Words of understanding
108 Helvetian
109 Swamp thing
110 First place

DOWN

1 Butler's last word
2 Hydrocortisone cream additive
3 Cartoon shriek
4 Pea jacket
5 Under states
6 Hebrew month
7 Mormons, initially
8 Ring around the collar
9 One that moves at a measured pace
10 Zsa Zsa's family
11 Dress with a flare
12 Verne's peripatetic hero
13 Small pocket
14 Flippers
15 South African township
16 Erelong
17 E-5 and E-6
18 Stand up to
24 Letter opener
26 Many PCs
29 Heavenly beneficience
32 Gibberish
33 Study piece
35 In concert
36 They may be carved in stone
37 Catlike Chinese leader?
38 Pier group
39 Shakespeare title character
40 Men behaving badly
41 Duck feed?
42 Court org.
43 Arafat
45 Mudville disappointment
46 Lowlife
49 1942 death march site
50 "Phooey!"
51 Stuck on
53 Tabby's treat
55 Bird with a ten-foot wingspan
57 Michelangelo masterpiece
58 Rudder locale
61 Beach wear
62 "Cheers" cast member
63 Prepared to fire
64 Made the cut
65 Internet destination
66 It's just part of an act
67 "Illumined Pleasures" et al.
68 Amor vincit ___
69 Mobile homes
72 More adept
73 Angle irons
75 Harasses hubby
76 Alex Webster was one
77 One way to win a fight
80 Kind of buddy
82 Broadcast news?
84 "Peter Pan" playwright
85 Polish wedding favorites
86 Meadow lands
88 Pawns
89 Earth tone
90 Where Timbuktu is
91 Roar of the crowd
92 Mass setting
93 Muslim mystic
94 Head over heels
95 Gave the once-over
96 Monique's mom
97 Apt name for a colleen
99 House work
101 A really big shoe
102 Written with two sharps

37 A GO-GO by James Connolly

110 Across is named after a village near Milan where it was first produced.

ACROSS

1 Math rules
5 Signs of healing
10 Give an edge to
14 Kaput
18 K–12
19 Patient's cry
20 Ship to Colchis
21 Kevin of "Dave"
22 Huge number
24 Amorous look
26 Sporty Ford, to car buffs
27 Help for disaster victims
29 Tens represent them
30 "Gil Blas" author Lesage
32 Seemingly forever
33 Tiny change on a graph
34 London landmark
37 Shoppe sign word
38 Cape in W Portugal
39 Dean's list fig.
42 Earth Day sci.
43 Nonsense
47 Western treaty gp.
48 Memphis river
49 Perry battle site
50 Footnote abbr.
51 Not "fer"
52 Multi-vol. reference
53 Rome's ___ the Younger
54 Many AMA members
56 Lloyd's Register data
58 Going from 2 to 6, say
60 Sketch out
61 Wawa's portrayer on 5 Down
62 Piece org.?
63 Wimbledon winner in 1971/1980
67 Shipping dept. stamp
68 Circus number, often
71 Bump on a log
72 Results
76 Antifungal cream
78 Merino mother
79 "___ Irish Rose"
80 "___ my brother's keeper?"
81 Become tiresome
82 Verdi slave
84 Some ensigns-to-be, for short
85 Keyed up
86 Grafton's "___ for Corpse"
87 "Taras Bulba" author
91 Alaric, e.g.
92 Bonzo, e.g.
93 From square one
94 Whistle time
95 Almanac sayings
97 Uses a scope
98 Beefeater et al.
99 Surgery tool
101 Hypo holder
104 Rotten advice
106 Places to rough it
110 Pungent cheese
112 Source of mohair
114 At full tilt
115 Amu Darya's outflow
116 On the lam
117 Oratorio number
118 Poor, as excuses go
119 Cribbage need
120 Krupp Works city
121 Be dependent

DOWN

1 Hamstring sites
2 Slews
3 Word to a nag
4 Ready for John Henry?
5 NBC skit show, briefly
6 Prefix for element #29
7 Senator Specter
8 Teacher's deg.
9 Ovum, e.g.
10 Went by Conestoga
11 Reform Party founder Perot
12 They may clash
13 Dress up
14 ___ apnea
15 Casual greeting
16 Scott Turow title
17 Skeffington in "Murder by Death"
21 Big bear
23 Make 24 Across at
25 Burnt umber, e.g.
28 Hacked it?
31 Actress Pier
33 Get on the ump
34 "Death ___ proud": Donne
35 Less congenial
36 Grimm fowl
37 Toe the line
38 Mil. unit
39 Armageddon combatants
40 Satchel in the Hall
41 Ed in "Sleeping Dogs Lie"
44 Kind of gasket
45 "Exactly!"
46 Type of question
51 W.R. Grace ___
53 Take second
54 Forest clearing
55 Hill gofer
57 Crack agents
59 2004 Super Bowl MVP
60 Yokemates' burden
64 Heat center
65 "It's ___ deal!"
66 "Ut" was one of his notes
68 Longtime Crosby label
69 Yellow primrose
70 Conductors, e.g.
73 Magnetic flux units
74 Ham it up
75 They're often heaved
77 Sound equipment
79 Egyptian god of life
83 Market index, briefly
85 Lab gel
87 Hit the ___ the head
88 "Peaceable Kingdom" figures
89 Electrolysis atoms
90 Lose freshness
96 Metric prefix
97 Saul Bellow's March
98 Forced labor camp
99 Plastic blocks
100 Emanated
101 ". . . ___ in Kalamazoo"
102 "The Starry Night" museum
103 Brit's buggy
104 Nudnik
105 Genesis grandchild
107 Seconds
108 McKinley's "full dinner ___"
109 Stiffener of sorts
111 Use a Taser
113 Nickelodeon pooch

38 HEARTLESS by J.P. Conway

As of 2005 the Jin Mao Tower (31-A) is listed as China's tallest building.

ACROSS

1 Reunion gps.
5 Czech mark
10 Doesn't swing at
15 One of a B-29's four
19 Nichols hero
20 Popped up
21 Potpourri property
22 Old World coin
23 Jazz legend of radio?
25 Conservative columnist in rehab?
27 Like a mountain road
28 Best of seven, e.g.
30 Fuse
31 The Jin Mao Tower has 88
32 Zebu genus
33 Las ___, NM
34 Very, musically
36 Box-office sign
37 Tailpipe fastener
39 "The Sopranos" restaurateur
42 Hollywood actress?
45 Spit out
49 "Tarnation!"
50 Baby talk
51 Dangerous mosquito
53 3-D medical exam
54 Hook shape
55 Hardly a big-shot editor?
60 Underling's assent
62 Ballerina Moira
64 Come after
66 [titter]
67 Serengeti cub
69 Key below Z
70 Talk insincerely
72 Meir who succeeded Eshkol
74 Breakfast spots
76 Odorous
79 Take the pulpit
81 Dancer who's a safe investment?
85 Winner's sign
86 Duke's conference
87 Capital on the Red River
89 Seek a treat
90 Nectar source
91 Fifth Avenue store
93 Actor currently popular?
97 Ugarte in "Casablanca"
98 Reduce to mush
100 Not aye
101 Tangle or disentangle
103 Sacrifice sites
106 Prepare to drag
107 Play doctor, e.g.
111 Diva Mitchell
112 Oven button
115 Full of ideas
116 Baseball/ football star?
118 Actor with a script?
120 Blues great Rush
121 Properly timed
122 Pigskin-shaped
123 It may be tiered
124 Chris of "Sex and the City"
125 Bikini event
126 Out of gas
127 Bauhaus artist

DOWN

1 Friday sought them
2 Friar's Club bigwig
3 Prefix with brew
4 RR transport ship
5 Saintly auras
6 Awakening
7 Some elephants
8 Conductor ___-Pekka Salonen
9 Grammy winner Alicia
10 Place for a brew
11 End of MGM's motto
12 Japanese beef
13 They'll never fly
14 Kind of bunt, on scorecards
15 Chump change
16 Like the futhark alphabet
17 Hold forth
18 Corn loaves
24 Oscar winner Rainer
26 Pitch
29 River of Aragón
33 Amusing island
35 Bard villain
36 Sporting brogans, say
37 All gone
38 Hunk's pride
39 Sidewalk stand buys
40 Devil-may-care
41 Meditative actor?
43 To boot
44 Sawgrass scores
46 Premier tennis star?
47 Euclid's lake
48 Informant's wear
52 Soft seat
55 Bring up
56 Gordon of the NBA
57 Little bird
58 From Cardiff, say
59 Echidna's prey
61 Try to sniff out
63 Turturro of "The Sopranos"
65 Farm stand units
68 In the offing
69 Boxers' org.
71 ___ Paul guitars
72 Student stats
73 Shamu, for one
75 Like Pindar's works
77 Warm, so to speak
78 "Runaway Bride" actor
80 They may be split
82 With adroitness
83 Heir, usually: Abbr.
84 Eisner's successor
88 Vane dir.
90 Hit the campaign trail
92 "Caramba!" origin
94 Israeli parliament
95 Gutter locale
96 Add one's voice to
97 Geordi on "Star Trek: TNG"
99 Caspian Sea feeder
102 Zigged and zagged
103 Illinois city
104 Resulted in
105 Namely, in legalese
106 Twin of myth
108 Rope fiber
109 Bring out
110 Adorée of silents
112 Pub purchase
113 Jim Dandy, for one
114 Pull a sulky, perhaps
115 Turn black
117 Mauna ___
119 IV squared

39 ET AL. by Richard Silvestri
How many Trekkers know the answer to 91 Across?

ACROSS

1 Lexicon look-up
5 "YOU are here" symbol
10 Violinist Zimbalist
15 "Hurry up!"
19 "The Morning Watch" novelist
20 Sheer fabric
21 Non ___ (unwelcome)
22 Richie Cunningham's wife
23 Almost a prayer book?
25 Romany plotters?
27 Shrink
28 Draws in
30 Limited
31 Walking stick?
32 Party gift
33 Shampoo problem
34 Really big shoe?
35 Judging group
36 Acts skittish
37 Luciano's love
40 Nor'easter flip-flop?
42 Suffix meaning "foot"
45 Kind of society
46 Shot of hooch
47 Duffer's dream
48 Intense
50 Munchkin kin
51 Matte's opposite
53 Supported
55 Very soon after
56 Come to a standstill
58 Dark
60 Empire State capital
62 Reluctant
63 AOL messages
64 Tasteless porridge
65 Until now
67 Improvises musically
68 Container for film
71 Defeat, slangily
72 Michaelmas flower
74 Bucket bracers
76 Devon river
77 Texas Hold'em stakes
79 Hard water?
80 Peerless person
81 Wield the shears
82 Sauce source
83 Academy taught by Olympic champions?
88 Altercation
89 Boy-meets-girl event
90 Cite verbatim
91 ___ Ka Ree (Vulcan Eden)
92 Steep slopes
95 Inflicts injury
96 Super Bowl XXXV site
99 Now
100 "Ode to Psyche" poet
101 British currency
104 Rubbish-filled waterway?
106 Florist's snit?
108 Daughter of Mnemosyne
109 Famous fountain
110 ___ fours (crawling)
111 Use a swizzle stick
112 CPR specialists
113 Gave a darn?
114 Ersatz vanilla bean
115 Presidents' Day event

DOWN

1 Vacuum cleaner attachment
2 Architectural curves
3 Do a double-take
4 Keister
5 Take to the air
6 "Lady Sings the Blues" star
7 Piece of high ground
8 Pay ending
9 City near Niagara Falls
10 Chinese food
11 A spring chicken
12 Séance communication
13 UFO crew
14 Fashionable London district
15 Trolley sounds
16 Exxon merger partner
17 Speechify
18 Frasier's brother
24 See 88 Across
26 Stanley Kubrick's art
29 Part of the eye
32 Sidewinder's weapons
33 Source of irritation
35 Take a breath
36 Break from the gate
37 Part of Hickok's hand
38 Brewer's grain
39 Garbageman's job?
40 A deadly sin
41 Louse up
42 Insect shelter?
43 School on the Thames
44 Say it isn't so
46 On the schedule
49 Ice and dice
51 Summer pest
52 Lip-smacking good
53 Nirvana
54 Breadwinner
57 Freak out
59 Shuteye session
61 Hall-of-Famer Aparicio
63 Studio accessory
64 Judicial knocker
65 "An autumn ___ that grew the more": Shak.
66 "Horrors!"
67 Chapel head
68 Dugout
69 Sign in the dark
70 Bank take-back
73 Staff members
75 Honey
78 Sully
81 Uniform in quality
84 Looks forward to
85 Sordid
86 Gruff
87 Where the action is
88 Quick-witted
89 Parsonages
91 "Streetcar" cry
92 Words on a Wonderland cake
93 Play a uke
94 Take it easy
95 Let fly
97 Madonna statue
98 Ear bone
100 Was familiar with
101 "The Man" Musial
102 Chew the fat
103 "Shall We Dance?" star
105 Live and breathe
107 "A Clearing" composer

40 BYE BYE BIRDIE   by John Greenman
Some of these puns are really out of bounds!

ACROSS

1 Get-up-and-go
6 Barn roof ornament
10 Hopping mad
15 Concrete square
19 Athenian square
20 Flair
21 Lloyd in "Airport"
22 Account
23 Duffer's lack?
25 Cutlass
26 Old Norse poetry anthology
27 Give the impression of
28 Daisylike bloom
29 Hacker tearing up the starting area?
31 Caldwell's "God's Little ___"
33 Turned a horse rightward
35 Spoonbill and boatbill
36 Winless horse
39 Pipsqueak: Var.
41 Dip accompaniers
43 Swashbuckler Flynn
44 Mania
45 Reconnaisance plane
46 Odin's realm
49 Painter Bakst
50 Glacial ridge
51 Long-armed ape
52 Tonsorial symbol
53 Leather factories
55 Trowel
56 River in SW New York
57 "Moon Mullins" cook
58 Pashmina ___
59 Sun-protected
60 Self
62 Duffer's ideal?
66 Droll
67 Principles
69 W Yorkshire city
70 Surpass
72 Infuriated
73 Helsinki natives
74 Felt melancholy
78 Levee
79 Summer camp craft
80 Abhors
81 Largest of the Inner Hebrides
82 Always, to bards
83 It's used in flares
84 Applied clapboards
85 Pastry chefs' aides
86 Standoffish one
87 Gladiators' togs
88 "New World Symphony" composer
89 Of the abdomen
92 What anglers do
93 Afrikaner
94 U.S. golf tournament time?
97 European ermine
100 Challenge
104 Tennis score
105 Counters
106 Play miniature golf?
108 Brainchild
109 Of the law
110 Tony's Off-Broadway cousin
111 Maternally related
112 Honeycomb compartment
113 With guile
114 D'Urbervilles girl
115 Eye sores

DOWN

1 Clods
2 Lascivious look
3 Pouting grimace
4 Star ballerina
5 Gave birth to
6 Doggerel
7 Came to rest
8 Basilica section
9 Invigorate
10 Foot part
11 Manned a dinghy
12 Sunburn soother
13 Piquant
14 Bestowing grants
15 Places
16 Serving spoon
17 Birch-family shrub
18 Grizzlies
24 Repair argyles
30 Record
32 "Snow White" collectible
34 Before, to odists
36 Dissolve
37 Kind of rug
38 Pro shop?
39 Ginkgo is one
40 Phone-service acronym
41 Bassinet
42 Use a strop
44 News source of yore
45 Vowel-stretching speech
46 Spoon maker?
47 "Luck and Pluck" author
48 Prepared
50 "Tosca" highlights
51 Gemstones
52 Degermark in "Elvira Madigan"
54 Vacate
55 Outbuildings
56 Greek consonant
58 Public disturbance
59 Porgies
60 Grain storehouse
61 Bottled-up one?
63 Poet Wylie
64 Gaseous element
65 Nuzzled
68 Make a boo-boo
71 Conflicting
73 Food and drink
74 Max Ernst's movement
75 Summers, to Simone
76 Jaguarundi
77 Rolltop
79 Hides
80 Something to write home about
83 Feather scarves
84 Titanic's plea
85 "___ Gotta Be Me"
86 Hereditary
87 With minuteness
88 Idolize (with "on")
89 Infant malady
90 Poetic form
91 Carpenter's tool
92 ___ point (hub)
93 Maine college
95 Genesis shepherd
96 Seasoned with a mint
98 Colgate container
99 Groucho's Driftwood
101 On the road
102 Rank
103 Gives the once-over
107 Legal matter

41 K-K-KATY by Norman S. Wizer
The song title has three K's.

ACROSS

1 Union foes
6 Imperialist of yore
10 Some TVs
14 Arctic birds
19 Feel grief
20 Mystique
21 Queen Noor's predecessor
22 Government security
23 Singer Gorme
24 "It Must Be Him" singer
26 Kind of candle
27 German camera maker
28 Ancient ascetics
29 "___ the motion!"
31 Journeymen?
33 Fidget
35 Golfer Se Ri ___
36 Candy-corn pieces
39 Southern broths served with corn bread
44 Bill Klem was a great one
47 Timesaving abbr.
49 Greek society
50 NYC's is approx. 41°
51 Goes under
52 Exemplars
55 New York mayor (1974–77)
57 Beasts of burden
58 Literary olio
59 Puppeteer Bil
61 Reveal
62 Ex-Bear Luckman
63 Regal Norse names
65 Genetic acid
66 Least animated
68 Madison Square Garden team
71 Lunchbox treat
75 "Mighty ___ a Rose"
76 Florida congressman Hastings
77 Cronkite's old network
80 Japanese beer brand
81 "Water Lilies" painter
83 Dough roll
84 Make fun of

85 Double-check property lines
88 "Rub-a-dub-dub, three men ___ . . ."
90 Baseball's "Hammerin' Hank"
91 "Is that Nikki with ___ or two?"
92 Novello of silent films
94 Song syllable
95 Bk. of the Bible
96 He does a balancing act?
99 Prospect
102 "How adorable!"
103 Summers on the Seine
105 Feast of Lights
109 Menu fish
113 ". . . made me ___ I couldn't refuse"
116 Sneering
117 Barrow
118 C.W. Post rival
120 Ringworm
121 Spanish rice
122 "A hand, a foot, a face, ___ . . .": Shak.
123 "Dies ___" (hymn)
124 "Since ___ for You": Lenny Welch
125 Oro y ___ (Montana motto)
126 Guiding spirit
127 Bugle call
128 Goddess of agriculture

DOWN

1 Small food fish
2 More demure
3 Murphy in "Destry"
4 Ceramicist's oven
5 Gym wear
6 Tap house
7 Genève locale
8 Asylums
9 Gathering tool
10 Tie 5 Down
11 "___ 1984" (Roddy McDowall film)
12 ENE, e.g.
13 Raipur raiment
14 Run of luck
15 Contrary to bowlegged
16 Man of Milan
17 ___ impasse
18 Dispatch
25 Part of FYI
30 Malice
32 Previous to
34 High-priced fiddle
37 Jeans label
38 Use a dirk
40 Black dog
41 Make joyful
42 Peace Nobelist José ___-Horta
43 Vein opener
44 NORAD trackees
45 Long skirt
46 Spotted
48 "Daily Planet" reporter

52 Dumbstruck
53 Monkee Jones
54 Kind of hole
56 Indifferent
58 Fashion model Wek
60 Frog genus
63 Walking ___ (ecstatic)
64 Flight test
66 1983 Mr. T film
67 Squeaked by
69 Rajah's consort
70 Stevedores' gp.
71 Chocolate substitute
72 ___ HOOKS
73 Leisurely stroll
74 Ankle-high shoe
77 Composer Nielsen
78 Patriotic fraternal org.
79 Town W of Troyes
81 Mr. Magoo, for one
82 Poi root
84 Platform dive
86 Regards
87 First mate
89 Greek cross

90 Kind of guitar
93 Shoots again
95 Geologic time division
97 African-American winter festival
98 Bridge boo-boo
100 Banana Republic company
101 Sweater sizes
104 Star of "Deadwood"
106 Pirate Hall-of-Famer Ralph
107 Designer Simpson
108 Snaps back
109 Give and take
110 Nobleman
111 Tourist stop in India
112 Played water polo
114 Move like a butterfly
115 ". . . my kingdom ___ horse!": Shak.
119 Ex-Red Ted's nickname

42 GO FISH! by Arlan and Linda Bushman
Nine fish are hiding in the grid below . . . how many can you identify?

ACROSS

1 Cash reserve
8 Keyboard key
13 L.A. WNBA team
19 Brideshead and Biltmore
20 Indian Ocean islands
22 Cantankerous
23 Taken by surprise
25 Body application
26 Joshes
27 Solid
28 Credit-card option
30 Ekberg in "War and Peace"
32 Delights
33 Jeane Dixon, supposedly
34 Small stock purchases
37 Worldly-wise
38 Taxing mo.?
39 Notice
43 Town official of old
44 Pen mate
45 Arnaz in "Forever, Darling"
47 Subway series site
48 Son of Odin
49 Great Chicago Fire scapegoat
55 Uncommon sense
56 Literary tributes
58 Crooked
59 Love song, maybe
60 Printer's proofs
62 Southern dessert favorite
64 Takanohana's sport
65 Bolt
66 Emcee bit
67 Many say there's no such thing
70 Strike out
73 Morocco capital
75 Kind of door
76 Papal interview
78 "Star Wars: Episode II" army
80 Prattle
81 Legendary Hun king
82 What 15 Down is
83 Pollster Harris
84 1973 John Houseman film
88 Jackie's second

89 Deal preceder
91 Novelist Grey
92 Nora Ephron's sister
93 Chop
95 Insightful
96 Short greetings
97 Long spell
98 Rattletrap
100 Norse goddess of beauty
102 Corsica neighbor
104 Dianne heard in "Robots"
105 National holiday of Mexico
109 Without
110 This, in Toledo
114 Roughly
115 Halle Berry's 2/27/05 role
118 Make the rounds
119 See 37 Down
120 Use the tape
121 Dour
122 ___ longlegs
123 Yagi namesake

DOWN

1 Narrow margin
2 Actor Morales
3 Tire cleat
4 Clutter-reducing event
5 Afr. nation
6 Work out
7 Launch wear
8 Grifter's art
9 "And ___!"
10 Friday's declaration
11 Incursion
12 Ringlet
13 Braze
14 Demonstrate
15 Scorpio's brightest
16 Pull (in)

17 McDonald's founder
18 Holiday song word
21 Silk Road city
24 Great Depression prog.
29 Savory jelly
31 Benchmark
32 Agree
34 Nautilus cousins
35 "None but the brave deserves the fair" poet
36 Quickest way, usually
37 Brat (with 119-A)
38 Dep.
40 Normandy Invasion's M4
41 Capital of Cuba?
42 Jabbers
44 Kitchen gadget
45 Solicit (business)
46 "I've got my ___ you!"
50 Gangsta ___

51 Fleet
52 Heap praise on
53 Tolkien baddie
54 "O ___ on Parnassus Hill": Burns
57 Kitchen wrap
61 Shaves
63 Check, in poker
64 Colorful shawl
65 Winningest NFL coach
68 Embry in "Timeline"
69 Guisewite strip
71 Hard to come by
72 More bizarre
74 Fire result
77 Kin to un-
78 Decked out
79 Isolated
80 Many E-filers
81 Wile E. Coyote's supplier
85 Online publication

86 Shankar offering
87 Outback runners
90 Connoisseur
94 Really focused
96 Gridiron get-together
97 Ready for takeoff
98 Ebert purview
99 Fall off
101 Generous one
102 Abated
103 Stretchy fabric
104 Card game
105 Sets a limit on
106 "Dies ___"
107 Parent's pre-homework directive
108 Witty remark
109 Energetic
111 Flabbergast
112 Fork-tailed flier
113 Expanse
116 Scepter
117 Polish off

43 INITIAL PUBLIC OFFERINGS   by Fran & Lou Sabin
The frater of 3 Down is lapsus calami.

ACROSS

1 Shows surprise
6 One way to get off
10 Meathead's meal?
15 Seckel's kin
19 Big splash
20 Naked archer
21 Introvert
22 Jumble
23 Class-A
24 Manic-depression
27 Man of Steel
29 Extensive accounts
30 He played 27 Across
31 "Ready ___, here I come!"
32 Pull a Peeping Tom
33 Hooey
35 Printing type
37 Jones of the Miracle Mets
38 Cheat sheet
39 Disc-brake part
40 Mooring site
41 Fisherman's hat
46 "Time After Time" lyricist
47 USS Virginia, for one?
49 Mah-jongg piece
50 Pale drink
51 Weighty matters?
52 It may be struck
53 Part of a three-piece suit
54 "___ a Small Hotel"
56 Bamboo piece
58 Dance of the Seven Veils dancer
59 Options
61 Single-masted craft
62 Money-raising effort
63 Sweeney Todd's town
64 Floribunda feature
65 Smallest number
66 Face reddener
67 Sigmund's sword
68 Literary accounts
69 Excellus coverage
72 Lip-puckering
73 Lose it
76 Dewdrop
77 Doctors do it
79 ___ in point
80 Come up
81 Lacking couth
82 Fern seed
83 Neck problems
84 It may be due
88 Hair pieces
89 It took the Overland route
90 Hawke of Hollywood
91 In advance
92 Anthropo-phagus
95 Arena in the "Marines' Hymn"
99 Cordwood measure
100 Jamboree housing
101 Prefix for plasty
102 Zip
103 Courtyards
104 Cinnabar and galena
105 Not in any way
106 Gave a kick
107 "Popeye" cartoonist

DOWN

1 Thous
2 Rights gp. founded in 1920
3 Lapsus linguae
4 William Carlos Williams epic
5 Of tougher stuff
6 Moroccan capital
7 Ugandan exile of 1979
8 KP tool
9 Miranda's father in "The Tempest"
10 Wine bottle
11 Navigation aid
12 Turns off
13 Small rorqual
14 "48 ___" (1982)
15 Sandhog's tool
16 "Here we are as in ___ days . . ."
17 Beachcombing tool
18 Pavin on the links
25 Furlough
26 Address the masses
28 Verbal gem
32 Duel provokers
33 Unfeeling type
34 Rob in "The Stand"
35 Whale that's a dolphin
36 Young mule
37 Snippy kids
38 "Prosit!" for one
40 Joyful sounds
41 Small porch
42 Goes flat
43 A hint of things to come
44 Perfume base
45 Find new tenants
47 Wake-up call?
48 Oneida Ltd. product
51 Architect's concern
53 They're changed on the highway
55 Seekers seek 'em
56 Replay mode
57 Mount in Deuteronomy
58 Clinched (with "up")
59 Tight grip
60 Ennoble
61 Model's forte
62 Misrepresent
64 Large family
65 "Not so!"
67 Float through the air
68 Bolshevik foes
70 Heist wear
71 Thomas Gray poems
73 Spin-off of the twist
74 Città of Vergil's tomb
75 Well-adapted subspecies
76 "Bebe" Bardot
78 Buttonquail's kin
80 Texas county
82 It's so sad
83 Small milk container?
84 Green pasta sauce
85 Not the same
86 Used a flashlight
87 Pielets
88 1:1, for one
89 Leslie Charteris sleuth
91 Letter run
92 Close-knit group
93 "Manon" highlight
94 Tragic king
96 ___ Ignacio de Loyola
97 Hawaiian menu fish
98 "Hernando's Hideaway . . . ___"

44   I LOVE NEW YORK   by Theresa Yves
38 Across may require a little thought.

ACROSS

1 Left
9 Treeless tract
15 Can't stomach
20 Put off
21 More sacred
22 Utopia keyboardist Klingman
23 Clever hula girls?
25 Extreme
26 Linear, for short
27 Decryption org.
28 Political slate
30 Where fig leaves were worn
31 Table d'____
34 Island state?
36 They have their ups and downs
38 Milk from the "Hey Diddle Diddle" cow?
42 Trapper's job
45 Photo lab abbr.
46 Phnom ____
47 Patient sounds
50 List shortener
51 Meadow sound
54 Diamonds, in slang
55 Prefix with morph
56 Stand
58 Bar output
59 Where drivers pull over
61 "Been there, done that"
62 Breaks off
63 Monitor clarity
64 "____ 'nuff!"
65 Gore and more
66 Where a jury gathers
67 Broad tie
70 Lanky "10" actress?
73 Moses' birthplace
74 Unwelcome e-mail attachment
75 "____ lazy river . . ."
76 Injection reactions, maybe
77 Post-grad exam
78 Perched on
79 Echo
81 River of Utah
86 Clearheaded
87 Appreciative of gasoline?
88 Muscat's land
89 "Seinfeld" uncle
90 Take a shot at
91 Western author Grey
92 Old Dixie org.
93 Prefix for care
94 Marshy area
95 Envelopes
98 Cad's confession?
101 Page of music
102 TV beatnik Maynard G. ____
105 Miniseries, often
106 Bad fellow in "Othello"
107 Life, for one
110 Georgia, e.g.: Abbr.
113 "Puppy Love" singer Paul
116 Country singer McCready
118 Fabric softener stock indicator?
122 Cell terminal
123 Feared fly
124 Personal account
125 Smart outfit?
126 Proficient
127 Kulaks

DOWN

1 Baylor University site
2 Zip
3 Half a round on the links
4 Hamstring, e.g.
5 At all
6 SMU's league
7 ____ all-time high
8 Longs
9 Doo-wop syllable
10 Kemo Sabe's friend
11 "Champion" of Spanish history
12 Smithereens
13 Exec extra
14 Gaelic
15 ____ Darya River
16 One of Henry VIII's Annes
17 Bugs showing off?
18 Shrek and others
19 Tatum's father
24 Jeanne ____
29 Tough boss
32 Prepares for the printer
33 Boots
35 Sound
37 Driveway blotch
38 Rabin's predecessor
39 Enough, for some
40 Golden Rule word
41 Flapjack franchise
43 Rib
44 On the line
48 Historian of Halicarnassus
49 Biol. or chem.
52 Make sense
53 Something of value
57 Sorrow signs
58 Folk legend Pete
60 Road company
64 Carroll character
66 Chase played by Kirstie
67 Cease, at sea
68 Indian instrument
69 Prehistoric pal?
70 Lighter fuel
71 First game
72 Future dam, perhaps
77 Cooper in "The Secret Garden"
79 Font option
80 Pro Bowl side
81 Cook book
82 Black cat, for one
83 Presidential runner of 1936
84 Thought-provoking
85 A Chaplin
91 Cover girl's cover-up?
96 Not seeing eye to eye
97 Kabob holder
99 Exxon, once
100 Where the Nile begins
101 "Common Sense" writer
103 Loses it
104 "Family Ties" mother
106 Muslim holy man
108 Matthew McConaughey movie
109 America's national flower
111 Instantaneous
112 Artist Magritte
114 Etta of old comics
115 Sacks
117 Thumbs-up vote
119 "The West Wing" prez
120 Watery expanse
121 Suffix with hero

45 MEMORABLE MOTS   by Nancy Nicholson Joline
"I don't even know what street Canada is on." — 60 Across

ACROSS

1 Columbia line
6 Illinois senator
11 Procession
20 Independent land since 1947
21 Olive and plum
22 Chowhound
23 "When I was a boy, the Dead Sea was only sick"
25 "Cauliflower is cabbage with a college education"
26 Corresponded
27 Cobbler's stock
29 Seattle-Phoenix dir.
30 "The Fountainhead" author
31 "___ De-Lovely"
33 "The Lion in Winter" star
36 Swamp
41 Fairy-tale opener
42 Electron tube
44 ___ the Elder (234–149 B.C.)
45 "If I were two-faced, would I be wearing this one?"
52 Beautify America target
54 Executing
55 Tempestuous
56 Preoccupied
57 Alter the evidence
59 "Walk On" producer Brian
60 "Vote early and vote often"
61 Write a cryptogram
62 Smooch
64 Tire catchers
65 Curb
66 Gorge
68 Layden of the Four Horsemen
70 1981 Diane Keaton film
74 Mineralogy sci.
75 "Crazy Legs" Hirsch
77 Emphatic type
79 "Directors are never in short supply of girlfriends"
83 "Tristan ___ Isolde": Wagner
84 Room for a change?
85 "Into Thin Air" setting
86 Maintain
89 70% of the human body
90 Aplenty
91 "We had a lot in common. I loved him and he loved him"
94 Jot
95 Ashcan School painter
97 Piece of cake
98 Stair post
100 Demand
103 Show that launched C. Chase
104 UV-A and UV-B
108 Foster child?
110 Only way from the South Pole
112 A certain kingdom
114 "A narcissist is someone better looking than you are"
120 "It's not bragging if you can back it up"
122 Yanqui
123 Lee's Gettysburg opponent
124 ___ larceny
125 Doctor's determination
126 Dropped the ball
127 Sheepish sign

DOWN

1 Churchill namesake
2 Russian lake
3 Deck
4 Hackneyed
5 Pundit
6 Wagering parlor: Abbr.
7 Audrey Hepburn's birthplace
8 Houston AHL player
9 Park of puzzles
10 Plus
11 Dot follower
12 Carole Maso novel
13 Experienced
14 Places of refuge
15 "___ Eat Cake": Gershwin musical
16 Corvine sound
17 United Airlines' org.
18 "Agnus ___"
19 Suffix for 110 Across
24 Minneapolis suburb
28 Ill-fated Genesis city
32 Channel for film buffs
34 Unctuous
35 Chaney of the silents
37 Malfunction
38 Rizzo who said "I'm walking here!"
39 Dutch painter Jan
40 Throng
41 Film starring 23 Across
43 Exciting
45 Chisanbopper
46 Famed frontiersman
47 Christina in "Cursed"
48 Trumpeter Weidinger
49 News bits
50 Generic
51 Gator's kin
53 "___ corny as Kansas in August . . ."
56 Democratic color
58 Niches
60 Militia
62 Word with fire or white
63 Essence
67 Rock's Oscar Night role
69 Fraternal hall
70 Morocco's capital
71 Send
72 Unpretentious eatery
73 Cicatrices
74 No couch potato he
76 Rock to sleep
78 Lion color
79 Initiated
80 Shaped like kiwis
81 On a lower deck
82 Edith Wharton's farmer
86 Cries of triumph
87 Ulyanov's adopted surname
88 Visor
91 Word appearing in sequels
92 Sallow
93 Religion of Bangladesh
96 Evans and 99 Down
99 "Alice" star
101 Battle of the ___ (1916)
102 More exact
104 Bill attachment
105 Name in violins
106 New England Bulldog
107 Skirt features, perhaps
109 Act targeting racketeering
111 "___ she blows!"
113 Chinese cabbage
114 Meander
115 Lake of Japan
116 Stephen in "The I Inside"
117 Energy unit
118 Young Darth Vader
119 ___ Alamitos
121 Club ___

SOLVE WITH E'S   by Fred Piscop
"Amelanistic" would be another clue for 100 Across.

ACROSS

1 Curly-tailed pooch
6 Creep along
10 Serenade the villain
14 Sweater letter
19 Bicentennial, e.g.: Abbr.
20 Lopez's theme
21 On a corvette
22 Rock's Van ___
23 Lena's vocal ability, slangily?
25 Down East doing?
27 Cheap way to travel
28 Puts a strain on
30 Lyricist Hart
31 PX patron, perhaps
32 Lady's man
33 Sierra ___ (Mexican range)
35 JFK's "109"
39 ___ beef
41 Flying formation
42 Pushrod pusher
45 "The Seven Year Itch" star
46 Bakery recipe change?
48 Vital statistic
49 Stir up
50 Junior dance
51 Cry out loud
52 Lift rider
53 It launched E. Murphy
54 Official French government auto?
58 Mimieux in "The Picasso Summer"
60 Weedy lots, e.g.
62 Blows away
64 Start of a pessimist's comment
65 Swahili's language group
66 Diagram, in a way
67 "You don't have to tell me"
69 Fern leaf
71 Pirate's companion, maybe
73 Cracker-spread meat
76 Deli pancakes
78 Tractor enthusiast?
80 Duct tail?
81 Netman's org.

82 Caustic alkalis
84 Just ___ (not much)
85 Gawk at
86 "Am ___ believe . . ."
87 New Hampshire optical center?
91 Ladybug's prey
92 It holds water
93 Author LeShan
94 Makes a point?
95 Outpourings
96 Pianist Watts
98 ___-poly
99 It's good to be under, at times
100 White elephant, e.g.
103 Jack up the stakes
105 0% APR deal, maybe
110 Oscar's Christmas dinner?
112 Untouchables do?
114 1993 NBA Rookie of the Year
115 Blue-pencil
116 Dancer's garb
117 Broadcasting
118 Places for plastic flamingos
119 Contradict
120 Album flaw
121 ___ Domingo

DOWN

1 Crowd sounds
2 Windsor, for one
3 Concerning
4 Antler part
5 Hellish
6 Architect Jones
7 "Fuhgeddaboudit!"
8 Browns, on scoreboards
9 House Speaker Dennis

10 Wheel runner
11 Author Dinesen
12 Earthquake
13 Japanese honorific
14 Something to prove
15 Le ___, France
16 "Auntie Mame" playwright Robert
17 Memphis loc.
18 1998 DreamWorks film
24 Diplomat's goal
26 Long in the tooth
29 A Brontë
32 "Blame It on the Bossa Nova" singer
34 State openly
35 As such
36 Like rope
37 Backside of Beauty?
38 Stadium cry
39 Some city dwellings
40 Lower in rank
42 Menu printer?

43 Reason to take bicarb
44 Postage dispenser
46 Put in alignment
47 Clotho, for one
50 Left at sea
52 Obfuscate
54 Magazine publisher Nast
55 "The Wreck of the Mary ___": Innes
56 Overthrow, e.g.
57 Take a bite of
59 Ivy-covered
61 Joltless joe
63 Dakota or Omaha
66 Radio button
68 Warm-hearted
69 Like Singh's swing
70 Dreads wearer
72 Mideast port
73 Snaps, slangily
74 Kate's TV friend
75 Bagel toppers
77 Iditarod racer
79 Hirsute

83 Orbital period
85 ___-Locka, Fla.
87 Dog breeders
88 Ed Sullivan offered it
89 Wall St. debuts
90 Picks out
91 With regard to
95 Fill beyond full
96 Quinn on screen
97 Chip away at
99 Provide lodging for
100 Off base?
101 Director Wertmüller
102 Shaped glass
104 Z ___ zebra
105 Sparkling vino
106 Smallville girl
107 "The Plague" setting
108 Plugging away
109 "Stoned Soul Picnic" composer
111 Multivolume ref.
113 Diving bird

47 "GO FIGURE!" by Jim Page
A clever challenger from a veteran wordsmith.

ACROSS

1 New voter
5 Sudden increase
9 Snowball fight sound
14 Salerno skills
19 ___-Chinese
20 Sheaf bristles
21 Emmy-winning Susan Lucci role
22 Ride at anchor
23 −11
26 "For example . . ."
27 Paris street
28 Top-Flite golf ball
29 ___ Lilly and Co.
30 Boom times
32 D-Day craft
33 Clothes-drying frame
35 They'll lead you on
38 "Tiny Alice" playwright
40 Tinsel hanger, e.g.
43 Kent State conference
45 "Tristan und ___": Wagner
48 −39 or −43
52 Port transport
54 Ban-___
55 Caen's river
56 "___ player that struts . . .": Shak.
58 Likely
59 Strong suits?
61 "___ be a cold day . . ."
63 London vans
65 Still-hunt
66 Nabokov novel
68 "___ of Blues": Presley
69 Full house, e.g.
70 −30
72 Mix a salad
76 "Mother ___" (old standard)
78 Catkins
79 Where run-off occurs?
80 Erodes away
82 Junction point
83 "I'm Not Lisa" singer Jessi
84 "Three Times ___": Commodores
85 ". . . by moonlight ___ window sung": Shak.
87 "Zounds!"
89 "Gidget" star
90 Auto accessory
92 −14 or −47
96 Torpedo
97 Cooler
99 Ancient Syrian city
100 1951 U.S. Open winner
102 Byzantine coins
104 Mollify
108 "Stay" singer Lisa
110 "Alias" heroine
112 "The Crying Game" star
113 Kind of fall
116 In favor
117 ". . . and ___ well"
119 +31
123 In an unclear way
124 Having 8 digits
125 Curling venue
126 Olympian hawk
127 Nasty look
128 Woody vine
129 Treats a sprain
130 Have the gumption

DOWN

1 Triple crown
2 Yawn producer
3 Lawn tool
4 Neither fish ___ fowl
5 Golden fabric
6 Bedside vessel
7 Give play-by-play
8 Air-pump letters
9 Douglas in "Aladdin"
10 Spin doctor's employer
11 Roman 52
12 Legal rights org.
13 Tropicana Field locale
14 Name that means "greatest"
15 +7
16 Resembling mosaic
17 Coup d'___
18 Nonmeat protein sources
24 Leaf-blowing, e.g.
25 Lapel-less jacket
31 French-cuff feature
34 Stirrup's place
36 Suzette's salt
37 1988 NL Rookie of the Year
39 Celestial giants
41 Dory movers
42 Rembrandt van ___
44 Radiator additive
46 Code sounds
47 Record producer Brian
48 Scintillate
49 Way to a man's heart?
50 "Cold Mountain" hero
51 "Hairspray" setting
53 Wine bouquets
57 Smoothed boards
60 +28
61 Type
62 Herbal tea
64 Pro player's agent
66 One-dimensional
67 Cotillion dance
70 Gagster
71 Chemical suffix
73 Eclipse
74 Longhorn
75 Make confetti
77 Washer brand
79 Calm, musically
80 Half court game?
81 "Snow White" (1967) author
83 Audrey's "Charade" costar
84 German gasp
86 Cement mixers
87 Like Earth's orbit
88 YMCA room
91 Pianist Bronstein Barton et al.
93 Beelike
94 Really cool
95 Trucker's locale
98 Bates in "Psycho"
101 Sleep aid
103 J.P. Donleavy novel
105 TV/radio union
106 Yokohama's Landmark ___
107 Uneven
108 Boys
109 Lena of "Alias"
111 Bette Midler's b'day
114 Painter Magritte
115 NASDAQ quotes
118 Mt. Hermon locale
120 Nitrilotriacetic acid
121 Ocean State school
122 Pillbox hat, e.g.

48 GO AND MULTIPLY   by Edgar Fontaine
Remember the title when you come to 26 Across.

ACROSS

1 "___ Rheingold"
4 Certain Prot.
7 Entertainer
14 Mover and shaker
18 Psi category
19 Uncertainties
20 Orange melon
21 Greene of "Bonanza"
22 Like skin after a facial
24 British police officers
25 Tries for a fly
26 A high probability
28 "___ Mame" (1958)
29 Highest trump suit in bridge
30 Entre ___ (confidentially)
33 Suit material?
34 Group of seven
37 Foot suffix
39 Intermission stats
41 Do a play
42 Employment summary
44 Stray
45 Visit
47 Ultraviolet source
49 Haydn wrote over 50
53 Catches (a bug)
54 Thug with heat
56 Muscle spasm
57 Spark-plug feature
60 Wobbly
62 Dullard
65 "That's right"
66 Passing notice
68 Soup du jour, e.g.
70 Socks and sundry
71 Imprecation
72 Scallion cousin
73 "Dance With Me" band
75 Rocker Nugent
76 Boa
78 They hunt in packs
80 Groan
82 Let up
85 Slip through the cracks
86 Smallest monkey
90 Major 2001 bankruptcy
92 Group of clans
94 Nothing-but-net sound
95 Nighty-night stuff
99 Past do?
100 Japanese religion
101 Celebes buffalo
102 Spider-Man co-creator Lee
103 Exploits
105 Roy Rogers' dog
107 "The Secret Storm" et al.
114 Director De Palma
115 Takeoff put-on?
117 Winning, at the casino
118 Three-time U.S. Open champion
119 DiCaprio film (with "The")
120 Not 'neath
121 We all do it
122 On pins and needles
123 Compactness
124 Source of some strange visions
125 "Awesome!"

DOWN

1 Politico Howard
2 City on the Tanaro River
3 "Wheel of Fortune" option
4 Wastrel
5 Financially solvent
6 False prefix
7 Places side by side
8 Great Barrier, for one
9 Seller's waste factor
10 Anglesey or Royale
11 Reddish brown
12 Pave the way?
13 Minnesota twins?
14 Sensible and practical
15 Rhetorician
16 Undivided
17 Fixes at zero, say
21 Baton Rouge school
23 Kind of Russian doll
27 Algonquian abode
28 Eventually
31 Not funny anymore
32 "Blue Book" bogies
34 Lose oomph
35 "Travels in Hyperreality" author
36 School-support org.
38 City on Lake Superior
39 Takes up
40 G.W. Bush title
42 Deliverance
43 Again and again
46 White lightning source
48 Cycles
50 Reading material?
51 Gladden
52 Cannonball along
54 Small lizards
55 Long stride
57 Scrooge's present to the Cratchits
58 Manila hemp
59 Flat breads
61 Had down cold
63 Alpaca kin
64 Domingo, for one
67 1978 hit by the Commodores
69 Timid
74 "Stealth" star
77 Baptismal bowl
79 "___ Fall in Love"
81 Kept in the dark
83 "Mending Wall" poet
84 Garrison
86 Hecate sorceress
87 Sermon subject
88 More than -er
89 Howe'er
91 Long in "love jones"
93 Hate-crime factor
95 Chatter
96 Hardened
97 Meting (with "out")
98 Cello leg
100 "Satisfaction" group
104 Bobbin
106 Joined up: Abbr.
108 Sleeveless Arabian garments
109 K2 creature?
110 On-air scheduling unit
111 Scary sound to a zebra
112 Pond growth
113 Flexible Flyer
115 Boy from the highlands
116 "Hail, Caesar!"

ANSWER GRID FORMULA   by Alvin Chase

Formula: 108A+18D−9D+86A−1A+61A+71A−95D+43D−14A = HOW YOU'LL FEEL!

ACROSS

1 Somerset Maugham story
5 Certain ski lifts
10 Hand-held organizers: Abbr.
14 "Five Weeks in a Balloon" author
19 Teen's trauma
20 Mongolian range
21 Enumeration
22 Like ___ in the headlights
23 Seneca and Shakespeare, e.g.
25 They take it to a higher court
27 Governing bodies
28 Sinaloa sandwiches
30 Not quite 100%
31 Tartan pattern
32 Of an eyeball area
35 Fortas and Saperstein
36 Vincent's loss at Arles
38 Make effervescent
39 Bean or Campanella
40 Business alias, for short?
43 Clinic employee
45 Owner
47 Sinbad's seven
48 Iniquitous spots
49 Kind of hold
51 Shinto shrine center
52 Highlands loch
53 Gasconader's suffix
54 Retaliation
59 U. of Maryland mascot
61 Bible Belt minority?
63 Peregrine's weapons
65 Irish Gaelic
66 Tech. schools
67 Rebel
68 Conehead's home?
70 Texas Hold'em chip
71 Slobber
72 Befuddled
75 Dolomite-like mineral
78 Science of antitoxins
80 Wrecker
81 Willed beneficiary
82 Whole lot (of)
83 Violinist Kavafian
84 Strike out
85 ___ serif
86 Got on board
92 Mandrake's girlfriend
94 URL suffix
95 Charlemagne's reign: Abbr.
96 Detective Lupin
97 The night before
98 Tear's partner
99 Smart shoppers
101 "Count wisdom ___ member of the war": Shak.
104 Accomplish
107 Exhausted
108 Be made up (of)
111 Brings back officially
113 Kind of speech
116 "The Guitarist" painter
117 Cartoonist Drucker
118 Major French river
119 Heart cherry
120 Luge and pung
121 Annie Oakley
122 Overindulges
123 Slips

DOWN

1 First Titanic deserters
2 Rural measures
3 Ridiculous
4 Naysayers
5 Nephrite
6 Ignorance, to some
7 ___ glance
8 Flowed
9 Thalia and Urania, e.g.
10 Mollify
11 Some radio antennas
12 Horned snakes
13 ___ Croix, Quebec
14 Sacramento, for one
15 Rotund cheeses
16 U. of Nevada city
17 Catches monarchs
18 At one time, once
24 Kett and James
26 Worker
29 River of Turkey
33 Frolic
34 Baritone Nucci
35 "Mighty Lak' ___"
37 Makeup exam
40 Firmly established
41 "Taxi War Dance" bandleader
42 NRA member
43 Snug retreat
44 Thoughtless
46 Watches baby
47 Used a springe
48 Dorothy's "Typhoon" role
50 Elects
54 Stairway part
55 Verona loc.
56 Teasdale and Lee
57 Still in the game
58 Weeper, proverbially
60 Settle a score
62 Enrols
64 Agrippina's killer
68 Noun suffix
69 Source of power
70 Close by
71 UPSed
73 "Nana" novelist
74 It sounds like you
75 "Now I see!"
76 Recurrent
77 Skin cosmetic
79 Longshoreman
84 Horse training
87 Ice-T and Ice Cube
88 Picks up
89 "The check ___ the mail"
90 Fruit juices
91 Jet-stream direction
93 ___-garde
95 Mob jobs
98 Unwaxed?
100 Locale
102 Forty-___
103 Tinseltown award
104 Sergeant at ___
105 Shade of blue
106 Trident part
107 Covered colonnade
109 Uncases, to Keats
110 Five make fifty
112 Stereo part
114 Two, in Klingon
115 Fold-up "sack"

50 CROSSWORD PUZZLE   by John M. Samson
The clue to this theme is in the diagram.

ACROSS

1 Crossword beginning
6 "Chariots of Fire" star
10 City SW of Bogotá
14 Like some picket lines
19 Precept
20 Muslim judge
21 Yemen neighbor
22 Wisdom ___
23 Miranda in "Tom & Viv"
25 Eel-like food fish
27 Corrida cheers
28 Taina in "Les Girls"
29 She fawns over fawns
30 Fixate
31 Necklace shell
32 Barrier-reef creations
34 Part of a sting operation?
35 Electric guitar pedals
37 Ashes holder
38 Texas Hold'em throw-in
41 "My Cup Runneth Over" singer
44 "The Gates of Ivory" novelist
48 Halcyon
50 Refrain syllables
51 "Faith of ___ Fathers"
52 Dawson in Super Bowl IV
53 Like Shepard's "Cowboys"
54 "Everybody must get ___": Dylan
55 Condi Rice's alma mater
56 Have a bite
57 Fallacious
58 She may fly the coop
59 Pueblo dwellings
61 Removes a stovepipe
63 Take a crack at
64 Data's daughter
65 South Korean president
66 Prefix for tax
69 Up until now
72 They're found below a skull
75 Kingston Trio classic
78 La Cosa Nostra
80 Deceive
81 Skin tone
82 Vatican souvenir
84 Outlook Express rival
85 Suffix for morph
86 Limonite, e.g.
87 Marsh rodent
88 Trainspotting site
89 Muscular
91 Curmudgeon
92 Bloomingdale's rival
93 Federal ID
94 Some take a bow
95 Accident-probing org.
98 Slung the mud
102 English
104 French cathedral city
106 Dawn deity
107 "___ got it!"
108 Weather-worn
111 Historic document of 1215
113 Zoologic medicine branch
115 Painter Durand
116 Scintilla
117 Aphrodite's consort
118 Toast type
119 Raison ___
120 Popular college sport
121 Apollo's symbol
122 Doll up

DOWN

1 Another, in España
2 Labourite Kinnock
3 Brain
4 "A Shropshire Lad" poet
5 Eugene T. Maleska book
6 A train?
7 Painting aid
8 City of Zambia
9 Stop sign holders
10 Julia Child's alma mater
11 "___ for the Misbegotten"
12 Ties that bind
13 Publicity
14 ___ manometer
15 Declassified
16 Swear, gesturally
17 Summers on the Riviera
18 Express mails, in a way
24 Stephen in "feardotcom"
26 Sea dog
33 Royal ball?
35 Cardiff citizenry
36 Have ___ with destiny
39 Come into (debt)
40 "Our Gang" dog
42 Where Zeno was born
43 Pony Express pouch
44 Two-times
45 Hägar's letter
46 Unfatty
47 Exalted
48 Confederate battle flag
49 Danube tributary
60 Skiff mover
62 Center of Chicago
66 Trick endings
67 Nyota aboard the Enterprise
68 "The Faerie Queene" hero
69 Shofar
70 Luggage brand
71 Ali Baba's utterance
72 Met, to a Yankee
73 Like streakers
74 "___ or salad?"
75 "Tic Tac Dough" host
76 Instant
77 Mysore maids
79 AquaBall, for one
83 His profits are mainly on paper
90 Tikkanen of the NHL
96 Kind of drum
97 MIT degree
98 Mattress name
99 Cycle race
100 "___ street's a boulevard . . ."
101 Dissuade
102 Spanish 1 verb
103 Gussy up
104 Make ___ dash for
105 "Welcome Back" hip-hopper
109 Kathryn of "Law & Order: Criminal Intent"
110 "Deathtrap" actress Cannon
112 German eel
114 Suffix for Siam

ANSWERS

FOREWORD

```
T O O T E R █ S O I R
O R N A T E █ C U T E
A S T R O S █ A T A N
D O O R █ T A M A L E
█ █ █ E S S O █ G I G
W A L D O █ N I E C E
H I E █ R E E L █ █ █
A R N E T T █ L A P S
L O O T █ H U B C A P
E U R O █ E V E N S O
S T E N █ L A T E S T
```

#1

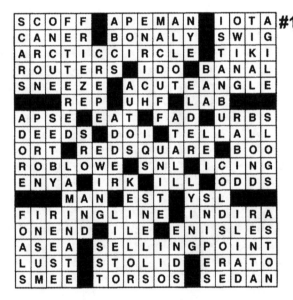

```
S C O F F █ A P E M A N █ I O T A
C A N E R █ B O N A L Y █ S W I G
A R C T I C C I R C L E █ T I K I
R O U T E R S █ I D O █ B A N A L
S N E E Z E █ A C U T E A N G L E
█ █ █ R E P █ U H F █ L A B █ █
A P S E █ E A T █ F A D █ U R B S
D E E D S █ D O I █ T E L L A L L
O R T █ R E D S Q U A R E █ B O O
R O B L O W E █ S N L █ I C I N G
E N Y A █ I R K █ I L L █ O D D S
█ █ M A N █ E S T █ Y S L █ █ █
F I R I N G L I N E █ I N D I R A
O N E N D █ I L E █ E N I S L E S
A S E A █ S E L L I N G P O I N T
L U S T █ S T O L I D █ E R A T O
S M E E █ T O R S O S █ S E D A N
```

#2

```
P R I S M S █ O T T E R █ M E N A
R E D C A P █ B E L L E █ E D E N
O L E A R Y █ J A C K L O N D O N
P E A L E █ P E C █ I G U A N A
J A M E S M I C H E N E R █ █ █
E R A S █ T A T █ R E V E R E N T
T N N █ W W F █ H I V E █ O V E N
█ █ F I T █ F A K E █ S L E E T
█ J E F F R E Y A R C H E R █ █
S H A V E █ O L E S █ S O X █ █
S O M E █ P O L K █ O P T █ S S N
R I B R O A S T █ E P A █ B E A U
█ █ █ U P T O N S I N C L A I R
A S S I Z E █ A C E █ H Y M N S
V I C T O R H U G O █ P E T I T E
E M U S █ E A T E R █ M A H L E R
R I T A █ D W E L T █ S P E E D Y
```

#3

```
M E D █ Z I P █ N E S T █ T S A R
A X E █ E O N █ A G E R █ A Q U A
I P L A N T E D S O M E █ S U N K
T A I L █ A U R A █ I M I T A T E
A N G L E █ M E L █ T O N E R █
I S H █ S H A W █ B I R D S E E D
S E T █ C O T █ T I C S █ J L O
█ █ N O L I M I T █ I D A H O
█ A B I R D C A M E U P N O W I
L E A P T █ █ C O R N I S H █
E R R █ I T A R █ W E T █ J A R
D O N T K N O W █ W E R E █ A M O
█ S H I N E █ V A L █ P I N E S
L A T I N O S █ O R C A █ R E N E
O D O R █ W H A T T O F E E D I T
B A R T █ A O N E █ M A T █ O T T
E M M Y █ Y E N S █ E R A █ E Y E
```

#4

```
C A F E █ S H I V █ K A I J U
U R A L S █ B A S E S █ A D M E N
E M I K O Y A M A N E █ T R A D E
█ B R E A M █ F I A N C E E █
P O I █ R A D I A T O R █ N E A T
O N E R S █ I S H I R O H O N D A
P E S O █ A G T █ C A P E █ G A L
█ █ B A B I E D █ █ R E L I C
█ O X Y G E N D E S T R O Y E R █
P O R N O █ █ W A H I N E █
U N A █ G A E A █ F E N █ T E G G
R A Y M O N D B U R R █ D O N H O
E S S O █ D I S R A E L I █ T I P
█ █ T R I N I A N █ G O U R D
O R T H O █ A N N I V E R S A R Y
A K I R A █ S T I N E █ S O D A S
R O D A N █ H A S T █ S A H L
```

Crossword grids (answers filled in). Black squares shown as █.

#5

```
S A L V O █ M U S T Y █ G E S T E
A T E I N █ A R N I E █ R A P I D
L E A P E R S S O N S █ O R A N G
E A V E █ E S A U █ O A K T R E E
█ M E R I T █ T O R N █ H E S S █
█ █ █ P R E S S O N S E A L █ █ █
█ E P I S O D E █ H O E S █ E A R
A M O C O █ E R A █ █ L E T S G O
M I L K █ A N A G R A M █ O S H A
P L A Y E R █ █ T A B █ P R O A M
S Y R █ O R C A █ V I S I O N S █
█ █ S O N A R S L E E P S █ █ █ █
M O E N █ Y I P E █ █ Y A N K S █
C O N F E S S █ T I N O █ I N C A
R O S I N █ P A R S O N S L E E S
A L E R O █ E X I L E █ P L A N K
E A S E S █ R E P E L █ F A D E S
```

#6

```
D E U S █ T O S E A █ B A D G E S
E S S O █ A H Y E S █ O T O O L E
P A S S I N G S C H O O L Z O N E
T U R A N D O T █ C O M █ E G I S
█ █ L E D █ L A Z █ █ O N A █ █ █
A B S C A M █ T A K E I T S L O W
P A P A W █ O R M E █ G R E █ █ █
A N I L █ P R O P █ █ L E T O U R
C A N C E L E D █ S C O T T I S H
E L A I N E █ W A C O █ E N T O █
█ U N A █ C A N S █ D E K E D █ █
B U R M A S H A V E █ C E S S N A
A P O █ █ I T E █ T I L █ █ █ █ █
I T S A █ P E C █ A C R E F O O T
L I T T L E S H A V E R S G R O W
E M E R I L █ U P O L U █ H U L A
D E R I D E █ P A W L S █ I S A S
```

#7

```
D A N C E █ A G A P E █ M A S T S
A M O U R █ N A T A L █ E Q U A L
K I S S A N D T E L L █ G U I L E
A G E S █ I R E █ L I B █ A T O P
R O S E █ M E L T █ S E R P E N T
█ █ D U B █ E H S █ G E L █ █ █ █
A H A █ F U D G E T H E F A C T S
C O M P O S E █ M O A T █ N A R C
E V I L S █ F L I P S █ X E N I A
R E N O █ T O O K █ T A R D I E R
B R O W N I E C A M E R A █ T D S
█ █ S O D █ I D A █ G Y M █ █ █ █
W A S H R A G █ O I L Y █ I L S A
I D E A █ L I P █ L O L █ M A I N
N O T R E █ J I M M I E S O P E N
G R I E R █ O C E A N █ U S A G E
S E N S E █ E A R N S █ M A Z E S
```

#8

```
L O S T I T █ I L S A █ T R A D E
A T E A S E █ N O T E █ S E R U M
N E T T L E █ C O A T █ E F R E M
C L O S E T E R M I N A L █ E T A
E L F █ █ H M O █ R A T I O S █ █
S O F A S █ O W N S █ M O T T O S
█ █ E L I █ D A T A █ T I G H T █
T A F F E T A █ T E N S █ S O A R
O B I █ W I N D U P T I P █ A R I
T I N S █ N O O R █ E A R F L A P
A D I O S █ D D A Y █ M I L █ █ █
L E S S O R █ G L E E █ M A R I O
█ H O R A C E █ A R S █ █ E N G █
A L B █ C H E C K R E C E I V E R
G A U Z E █ L I E N █ A C T I V E
O T T E R █ E T R E █ T H E S E S
G E T B Y █ B Y R D █ S O M E R S
```

#9

```
█ S P O O R █ M E T R O █ L A R K
S H E P H E R D M E A D █ O D O R
H O W T O S U C C E E D █ G O B I
H O S E █ A L I E N █ S T A R E S
█ █ D O L E █ E S S █ I N E R T █
C A L █ V E R A █ T A P █ S T Y █
E R A S E S █ S P O R T I N █ █ █
L E M O N █ S T O N E R █ E R M A
I N B U S I N E S S W I T H O U T
E A S T █ M A R T I N █ W R O T E
█ █ H A I R N E T █ S A U T E S █
T V A █ S T E █ E V E N █ S S T █
R A N T S █ D I M █ I N G A █ █ █
E L N I N O █ S I E N A █ B R O M
B L U E █ R E A L L Y T R Y I N G
L E A R █ F R A N K L O E S S E R
E E L S █ F A C E S █ R O S E S █
```

#10

```
P A C T █ A M I G O S █ A M A S S
O D O R █ R A R E L Y █ C O U P E
H E M I S P H E R E S █ A L T A R
L E A S H █ N A S T █ D E U C E █
█ █ T A L K E R █ E W E █ M E N █
J A N E D O E █ D E M I M O N D E
U G O █ S W A P █ A S T I R █ █ █
D E R M █ I N L E T █ █ A I M T O
A N T I █ Q U A V E R S █ B R E R
S T E A D █ S E R U M █ I B M S █
█ M A X I M █ Y S E R █ I P O █ █
S E M I F I N A L █ S L O E G I N
O X O █ T I C █ Y I E L D S █ █ █
N O P U N █ I N N S █ E C O N O █
O D I L E █ S I X T Y F O U R T H
R U S E S █ O C E L O T █ D A W N
A S H E S █ R E S E N D █ O N T O
```

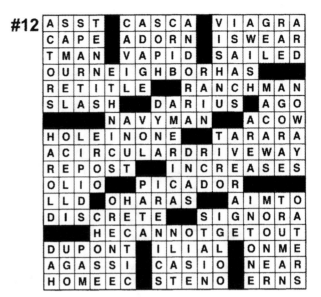

#11

#12

#13

#14

#15

#16

#17

```
L E W D   C A S A   N A M E   W A R D
A C H E   O D O R   O V I D   O G E E
T H I N G S D O C O M E T O   R I D E
H O R S E M A N   R A R E   F L O O D
      N I X   O L D S   S O D
A L C A I C   T H O S E W H O W A I T
H O R D E   C O O P   E A T A B L E
E L U L   P A Y   A B E D   R O S A
M A X I M U M   A R C A D I A   Y A K
      B U T O N L Y T H I N G S
M A C   D A M A G E S   E G O T I S M
A L L A   T I N A   A S S   R A T A
U T E N S I L   O B I T   C U M I N
L E F T O V E R F R O M   H O M B R E
      I R E   E L A N   B U Y
C R U D E   S P A T   D I S P O S A L
E U R O   T H O S E W H O H U S T L E
D E N T   N A S H   T O M E   L O I N
E R S E   T H E Y   O W E D   O P T S
```

#18

```
F O N D O F   I T S P A T   P A R O S
A M O R A L   C A T A L O   E M I L E
L A W O F A V E R A G E S   D E C A L
S N I P   I R A T E   S P I N O F F
E I N   E A T S   U R S U L A
      A L B A   T E S T P A T T E R N
B A L L V A L V E   A S T R O B O Y
E X O T I C   E N O S   H I R E O N
D E T O N A T E   S I A M   C O R K Y
      B A R H A R B O R
C E L E B   I S A K   O N E O N O N E
O S I R I S   M A R V   S C E N I C
M A N I T O B A   T O R C H S O N G
B U C K P R I V A T E   E A R S
      L E G A T E   V A N E   V E T
C H I C A N O   T E P I D   A I D A
R E L A Y   T H I N G S Y O U P A S S
I R E N E   R E C E D E   O M E L E T
B O X E R   Y E A R N S   H A S S L E
```

#19

```
S P A S   S T A R   B A R R   C A L F
A L G A   L A N A   E C H O   O L E O
F O O L H A R D Y   F R O S T B I T E
E D G I E S T   P I E   A I R
      N A H   A B E T   P L E A S E D
C O W E R   E R O S   L A I R   T A O
A B E   T O Y E D   R E I N S   O S S
R O S A   G R A Y B E A R D   K N E E
R E T I R E E   A D D S   H E E D S
      I D E E   C H A O S   V I E W
D E N E B   B R A E   S E E P A G E
O L D S   P O U N D C A K E   S L A B
T A I   F L U E D   Y E A S T   L I B
E T A   E A R L   D A R T   R E S T S
R E N D I N G   D I N O   C U R
      U N A   G U M   D O N A T E E
G U E S T R O O M   Q U I C K S A N D
A M A T   I D E M   A R N O   E R I N
S P R Y   A E R Y   F I G S   D A D A
```

#20

```
B E S E E C H   G A G A   S I M P E R
A T T A C H E   E X A M   C R E O L E
T H E S C I E N T I S T C R O S S E D
T E P E E   D A I S   H O N   T V A
Y R S   K E P T   A M I D   F E E T
      P A N D A   N E A T   B O R N E
G U I D O   E C O N   A R C
A S E A B I R D A N D A D A I R Y
B E E R Y   S A G A   I N D Y   I I I
O L D S   F A D E   A N T S   A B E T
P I T   A L A I   A R G O   A M B L E
C O W B E C A U S E O N E G O O D
      H U E   T R I S   Y A R N S
A S H O T   T O G A   B A R R E
V E E P   A A R E   S I T E   S A P
A V A   A L P   O P A L   D I E G O
T E R N D E S E R V E S A N U D D E R
A R T I E R   L E A N   S E A L A N T
R E S E N T   M O L D   T A L E N T S
```

#21

```
R E A M S   E T T A   A M M O   T C M
O N T A P   L E H R   M A R K   H U A
B Y T H E T I M E A M A N I S   O T C
S O A R E R   P A G O D A   C R A B
      E D A M E S   S E T I   H E R E
D P O   I I I   S A U E R K R A U T
R E D C E L L S   W I S E E N O U G H
A L D A S   I L I A C   P O M
W O M B T O T O M B   S T E W A R D S
U T A   V I T A   D O R A   A R A
P A N A C E A S   T O W A T C H H I S
      P A R   N O S E D   A I R E S
S T E P H E S T O O   D E G R E A S E
T O U R N A M E N T   I O R   H T S
E B R O   T O N O   A N N O Y S
F L A X   L U N A T E   D A C R O N
A A S   O L D T O G O A N Y W H E R E
N M I   C L E O   I M R E   A M E B A
S E A   S S R S   O S S A   Y O K E L
```

(BILLY CRYSTAL)

#22

```
B R A S S   A G A P E   L A R C H E S
L E D T O   N L E R S   O N E C E N T
O S I E R   T O R I C   D O G R A C E
W H E N E V E R Y O U F I N D   R I P
I O U   I C Y   R D A   S O N O
T E X T U R E   Y O U R S E L F O N
      B R I D L E   S N I P P Y
T H E S I D E O F   A C R O S T I C
R A S P   A L A N   K I X   R M S
A R T   T H E M A J O R I T Y   A P P
W P A   R A P   T A R E   E L E A
L O B B Y I S T   M A R K T W A I N
      A S T O R S   S P E E D O
I T I S T I M E T O   D E S K S E T
R A N K   E R N   A I N   E N O
I L S   P A U S E A N D R E F L E C T
S K I M A S K   A B O D E   L O F A T
I T S A L I E   M E D O C   A R I S E
N O T I O N S   S T E N T   P E T E R
```

Crossword puzzle solutions.

#23

```
HOBNOB . PASTA . SPRYER
ONEEYE . ALOUD . TIESTO
MIDDLEGROUND . ALIENS
ENS . TATTLETALEGRAY
. JOLLY . ORION .
FIGURE . ABS . CNN . OWE
EDENS . INDUTCH . SNOW
LETGO . CASBAH . ELAINE
TOOL . GES . BRA . ALLOTS
. VEGETABLEGARDEN .
ONEGIN . LIE . RNS . GREW
LARYNX . LOGSIN . DOILY
GRIM . BYTURNS . CENSE
ACT . CSI . AMA . GORGES
. SAUNA . AEONS .
LITTLEGREENMEN . SOU
ONHOLD . DURABLEGOODS
COULEE . ORATE . BERNIE
ORDERS . ROTOR . YESYES
```

#24

```
BLOWS . ABASH . BENELUX
RIVET . AORTA . INEXILE
AMERICANONION . JEWELER
GENERA . GOOD . ORESTES
. BOOTLIQUOR .
MAILBAG . INT . ADBIZ
ALLYBLONDE . IDS . RODE
REINK . DER . SPEC . YOLK
SCENIC . MASC . ARF . BEE
. ENDSOFTHEFALL .
HAD . GRO . TAOS . GEISHA
ALEE . OHMY . OTT . ETAIL
JOLT . MOO . ALEINCOURT
JUICE . LEX . NOENDTO
. DADDYLONGS .
JAWLINE . ERIE . EQUATE
INHASTE . COLEREUNION
BOUDOIR . USEDA . ADDTO
EXPENSE . PERSE . DOSES
```

#25

```
PERSE . BOBS . HOP . AFEW
ICEAX . IMAN . OHO . NODE
COLLE . GEBOARDS . GRID
SLYER . TRY . DRAT . LETS
. SCOOTS . LORELEI .
NEATIDEA . DIRNDL . GAP
ATLASES . WEBS . BENCH
BULGE . AILS . PRESLEY
SIE . SABLE . TREATERS
. BATTLE . GROUND .
RIGAGAME . GRUMP . GAS
ADORERS . PARE . HAITI
GOREN . BETS . PROLONG
ELI . TRALEE . ZEROINON
. CASELAW . SEARLE .
SEAT . DOZE . HAH . INSUM
ARLO . SHEERELE . GANCE
KILN . EAR . NEON . ATOLL
SKYE . ASS . ANTS . NEWAT
```

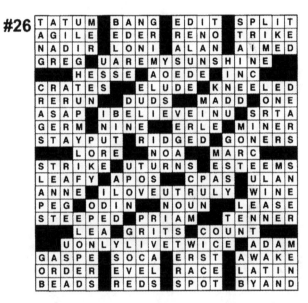

#26

```
TATUM . BANG . EDIT . SPLIT
AGILE . EDER . RENO . TRIKE
NADIR . LONI . ALAN . AIMED
GREG . UAREMYSUNSHINE .
. HESSE . AOEDE . INC .
CRATES . ELUDE . KNEELED
RERUN . DUDS . MADD . ONE
ASAP . IBELIEVEINU . SRTA
GERM . NINE . ERLE . MINER
STAYPUT . RIDGED . GONERS
. LORE . NOA . MARC .
STRIKE . UTURNS . ESTEEMS
LEAFY . APOS . CPAS . ULAN
ANNE . ILOVEUTRULY . WINE
PEG . ODIN . NOUN . LEASE
STEEPED . PRIAM . TENNER
. LEA . GRITS . COUNT .
UONLYLIVETWICE . ADAM
GASPE . SOCA . ERST . AWAKE
ORDER . EVEL . RACE . LATIN
BEADS . REDS . SPOT . BYAND
```

#27

```
ARNE . MANTA . CLASH . NEAT
LEON . UNION . OUTTO . ILWU
EDITHBOLLINGGALT . NOON
REDSEA . ETON . DOMICILE
TEE . DRIN . ERAS . IDO
. MARGARETMACKALLSMITH
. HEKATE . SIMAK . PROM
SOWED . TAME . MOI . SOILS
UVEA . DOLLEYPAYNETODD
MAL . LOWE . REAS . ARP
OLDSOANDSO . SKIPSASTEP
. ERN . APES . WEED . ONA
. MAMIEGENEVADOUD . LAZY
DELIS . ALT . ATON . DODOS
OGEA . REHAB . STROUD
JACQUELINELEEBOUVIER
. UFO . ALEX . ETTE . LEX
PGRATING . ANTS . STROBE
FLIT . LETITIACHRISTIAN
COSI . EVOKE . NAMED . ESTO
SPEC . DESOD . TROVE . SEEN
```

#28

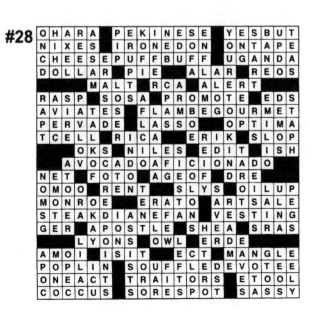

```
OHARA . PEKINESE . YESBUT
NIXES . IRONEDON . ONTAPE
CHEESEPUFFBUFF . UGANDA
DOLLAR . PIE . ALAR . REOS
. MALT . RCA . ALERT .
RASP . SOSA . PROMOTE . EDS
AVIATES . FLAMBEGOURMET
PERVADE . LASSO . OPTIMA
TCELL . RICA . ERIK . SLOP
. OKS . NILES . EDIT . ISH
. AVOCADOAFICIONADO .
NET . FOTO . AGEOF . DRE
OMOO . RENT . SLYS . OILUP
MONROE . ERATO . ARTSALE
STEAKDIANEFAN . VESTING
GER . APOSTLE . SHEA . SRAS
. LYONS . OWL . ERDE .
AMOI . ISIT . ECT . MANGLE
POPLIN . SOUFFLEDEVOTEE
ONEACT . TRAITORS . ETOOL
COCCUS . SORESPOT . SASSY
```

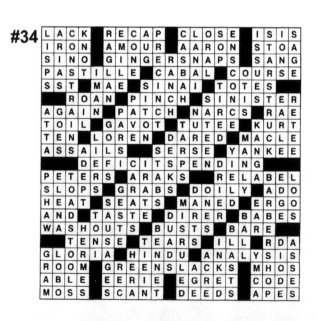

#29

```
SPATS  SLAT  AGATE  EVES
AURAL  PACE  DOZEN  TODO
STINE  ARID  DATEDEALER
STANDARDDIP  DETERGENT
      EDS  SUES  CHASE
ACCRETES  MEET  RAREST
NAH  DUCTS  PARTB  TEACH
ORI  THETA  MORITZ  GAI
RON  JEOPARDYTAKE  BLTS
ALFIE  SITE  YERTLE
KEENERS  RECAP  LIEOVER
  ADROIT  ASIS  AGILE
TITO  DRIBBLECHECK  SIP
ABU  FEELER  AKELA  ICE
CARPE  DELED  SEERS  OIL
TREATS  LARK  TENCENTS
    NIELS  DUET  AOL
ASSISTANT  BARRELFAULT
DUTCHSPEAK  TOOL  FIRER
AMOK  USENO  OVUM  ANISE
MOPY  PERKS  NETS  TESTY
```

#30

```
BART  AGES  IMAM  SPIRIT
ONEA  FOLK  NADA  ALSACE
OKCHORALE  DEARSTALKER
SLOOP  TIPPI  PIE  SEETO
TENETS  STAR  TAROT
    SEC  IRATE  AREOLAS
HECK  ERECT  WRAPARTIST
OCHO  PET  EMI  WET  HAHA
WHINESANDDINES  OPENER
LOCAL  MAI  AGA  RAREST
    MISSED  ESSAYS
STAMEN  GEE  EER  SLAVE
TATARS  HOSTELTAKEOVER
EXIT  USA  EAN  UMA  MORI
VILEPLAYER  TAPIR  ANON
ESTORIL  STARR  SAW
    ENACT  PECS  TOPEKA
IOWAS  ARE  REAPS  LOVER
SKIPTOMYLOO  DEEPFRIAR
MINION  ELAN  INRE  ETTA
SEDANS  RATS  ADEN  SASS
```

#31

```
COMO  LIBRE  STRAP  DEWS
AKIN  EDSEL  AROMA  ELIA
KARENBLACK  HOWARDFAST
EYESORE  SHAVE  TRALEE
  ITURBI  ORE  SIAM
MALDEN  INTRA  JACKEDUP
ULEES  ALCOA  TULLE  APE
READ  GULAG  SIDLE  ARTE
ARR  BURY  STINGY  ALLOT
LONGBEACH  ANTE  ARLENE
  ERGS  REFUSER  LOAN
ALDOUS  YELP  DOPESHEET
BEHAN  ASLEEP  YORE  HMO
ROAN  SITED  ROBOT  PAIN
ANN  RADAR  LITER  PERLE
MEDIEVAL  PIETA  CARDED
  SHAN  PLO  ONRAMP
USFLAG  KRONE  INPEACE
PHOEBESNOW  DYANCANNON
TORT  REESE  GUNGA  DKNY
OWES  YAWED  ELTON  SHEA
```

#32

```
TIER  BLARE  RAISA  SMOG
ADZE  LIMOS  ANNAN  TYRA
GOINSOUTHPACIFIC  EGAD
SLOOPS  SEINES  LOANING
    WEST  ADDS  ENGORGE
BRONCOBILLYBUDD  AGLET
REO  MAME  YEA  WISC
ANZAC  AARP  NEIN  RUR
SOYLENTGREENCARD  SALE
    ADORE  SEER  RESIZED
ACCRETE  STRAY  ONEEYED
DRUMSUP  ROAR  FLEER
OURS  RAGINGBULLDURHAM
SEL  ANNA  EYRE  MAUVE
    YVES  ESS  EACH  GET
NOTER  FATCITYSLICKERS
EROSIVE  ARCO  UPON
UMPTEEN  REUSES  POOLED
TOGA  ENDLESSLOVESTORY
ELUL  RESIN  ELLIS  TOMA
RUNS  SLOTS  SADAT  STAN
```

#33

```
TANGOS  OTHERS  ABSALOM
ALERTS  SHILOH  TORNADO
CONAIRAMERICA  TRIADIC
HUEVO  LOFT  ALCAN  YES
    ESPOSO  LORELEI
COOLEYHIGHNOON  OUNCES
ALB  LAS  EASTER  IDEAL
REECHO  PROM  YEGG  ASA
PUSHINGTINMEN  CRINGED
SMEAR  EER  INABAR  UELE
    PELTERS  TURNRED
LOGE  ARMIES  GEE  LITHE
UTILIZE  PATCHADAMSRIB
TAJ  RYAN  FEAT  TOMATO
ERASE  LAMARR  NCO  PUN
SUNUNU  FUNNYGIRLHAPPY
    EMERITA  OCELOT
CUE  GRAMM  ARKS  SEGAL
OLYMPIA  MOBYDICKTRACY
GERAINT  AVALON  EERIER
SEEPAGE  REHANG  GLENDA
```

#34

```
LACK  RECAP  CLOSE  ISIS
IRON  AMOUR  AARON  STOA
SINO  GINGERSNAPS  SANG
PASTILLE  CABAL  COURSE
SST  MAE  SINAI  TOTES
  ROAN  PINCH  SINISTER
AGAIN  PATCH  NARCS  RAE
TOIL  GAVOT  TUTEE  KURT
TEN  LOREN  DARED  MACLE
ASSAILS  SERSE  YANKEE
    DEFICITSPENDING
PETERS  ARAKS  RELABEL
SLOPS  GRABS  DOILY  ADO
HEAT  SEATS  MANED  ERGO
AND  TASTE  DIRER  BABES
WASHOUTS  BUSTS  BARE
  TENSE  TEARS  ILL  RDA
GLORIA  HINDU  ANALYSIS
ROOM  GREENSLACKS  MHOS
ABLE  EERIE  EGRET  CODE
MOSS  SCANT  DEEDS  APES
```

Crossword answer grids.

#35

```
TRIAGE   TOGAS    ROOM   MIR
HILTON   ENACT    ADHERETO
IFYOUCANTSAY       HINTEDAT
STARR   STOOD   DRNO   MILA
     MOPS   HEDDA    TACIT
RAISERS   SOMETHINGNICE
ORNATE   SELES    VOID
NACL  GAPE   ITSELF   STA
ABOUTAMANOR   ROSA   BURT
   STONES   DEMON   TENOR
OCTAGON   WOMAN   OCEANIA
TOURS   MERIT   ELLERY
INMY   ASIA   THENDONTSAY
SSE   ASWARM   MOST   RITA
   ASTA   ANAIS   TRADER
ANYTHINGATALL   DEEPEND
LOEWE   UNTIL   LADD
ESAI  ICET  ROWED  CRIED
AIRLINER   VOWOFSILENCE
SELLSFOR   EBERT   MANCHA
TRY  HOSE  GIDDY  PYTHON
```

#36

```
DAYS   CELLI    GAFFS   SAND
ALEE   OLDEN    ALOOP   ONCE
MOOEDMUSIC   BIGBADWOOF
NEWDEAL   HMONG   TEENSY
   PAS   BEWARE    ULT
ARMOR   BATONS   COLLOQUY
SUED   COBURN   SAGAS   USA
ONO   BAAEDMANNERS   PALS
NEWCASTLE   EASE   CACTI
ESTATES   PARKAS   OSKAR
   STAY   SWIFTER   ANTE
HYENA   SHEETS   DIDEROT
EATIN   CANT   ALAMODOME
WHUP   HEDDAGOBBLER   ANN
EON   BENET   INLAID   ATIT
DOGBONES   PAPERS   LISAS
   ASP   HONORS   OER
MONROE   SOLTI   ACADEME
ALARMCLUCK   NEIGHSAYER
LEVI   KAFKA   TENOR   TERI
ISEE   SWISS   SEDGE   EDEN
```

#37

```
LAWS   SCABS   WHET   SHOT
ELHI   NURSE   ARGO   KLINE
GOOGOLPLEX   GOOGOOEYES
STANG   REDCROSS   IDEALS
   ALAIN   EONS   BLIP
BIGBEN   OLDE   ROCA   GPA
ECOL   GOBBLEDYGOOK   OAS
NILE   ERIE   ETAL   AGIN
OED   PLINY   GPS   TONNAGE
TREBLING   PLAN   RADNER
NRA   GOOLAGONG   RCD
DOGACT   NODE   OUTCOMES
EXODERM   EWE   ABIES   AMI
CLOY   AIDA   MIDS   AGOG
CIS   NIKOLAIGOGOL   GOTH
APE   ANEW   NOON   ADAGES
   AIMS   GINS   LASER
AMPULE   BUMSTEER   CAMPS
GORGONZOLA   ANGORAGOAT
AMAIN   ARAL   LOOSE   ARIA
LAME   PEGS   ESSEN   RELY
```

#38

```
FAMS   HACEK   TAKES   PROP
ABIE   AROSE   AROMA   EURO
CBCALLOWAY   PTBUCHANAN
TORTUOUS   SERIES   UNITE
STORIES   BOS   CRUCES
   ASSAI   SRO   UBOLT
ARTIE   LATHOMPSON   SPEW
DAMN   GOO   AEDES   MRI
ESS   BBWOODWARD   YESSIR
SHEARER   ENSUE   TEHEE
   LIONET   ALT   PALTER
GOLDA   NOOKS   REEKING
PREACH   CDCHARISSE   VEE
ACC   HANOI   BEG   PEAR
SAKS   INMCKELLEN   LORRE
   PUREE   NAY   RAVEL
ALTARS   REV   REVISER
LEONA   PRESET   CREATIVE
TDWILLIAMS   RXHARRISON
OTIS   ONCUE   OVATE   CAKE
NOTH   ATEST   TIRED   KLEE
```

#39

```
WORD   ARROW   EFREM   CMON
AGEE   VOILE   GRATA   LORI
NEARMISSAL   GYPSYCABAL
DECREASE   LURES   FINITE
STILT   FAVOR   TANGLES
   EEE   PANEL   SHIES
AMORE   SANDALSTORM   PED
CAFE   SLUG   PAR   ACUTE
ELF   GLOSSY   BORNE   UPON
STAGNATE   UNLIT   ALBANY
   LOATH   EMAIL   GRUEL
TODATE   VAMPS   CANISTER
WHUP   DAISY   STAVES   EXE
ANTES   ICE   ONER   SNIP
SOY   MEDALSCHOOL   SETTO
   MIXER   QUOTE   SHA
ESCARPS   HURTS   TAMPA
ATONCE   KEATS   STERLING
TRASHCANAL   PETALPEEVE
MUSE   TREVI   ONALL   STIR
EMTS   SEWED   TONKA   SALE
```

#40

```
OOMPH   VANE   IRATE   SLAB
AGORA   ELAN   NOLAN   TALE
FLUIDDRIVE   SWORD   EDDA
SEEM   ASTER   TEETOTALER
   ACRE   GEED   WADERS
MAIDEN   TWIRP   CHIPS
ERROL   CRAZE   DRONE   WAR
LEON   ARETE   ORANG   POLE
TANNERIES   SPADE   TIOGA
   MAMIE   SHAWL   SHADED
EGO   PAREXCELLENCE   WRY
TENETS   LEEDS   OUTDO
ANGRY   FINNS   DESPAIRED
PIER   CANOE   HATES   SKYE
EER   BORON   SIDED   ICERS
   LONER   TOGAS   DVORAK
CELIAC   FISH   BOER
OPENSEASON   STOAT   DARE
LOVE   ABACI   PUTTERAWAY
IDEA   LEGAL   OBIE   ENATE
CELL   SLYLY   TESS   STYES
```

Completed crossword grids (answers).

#41
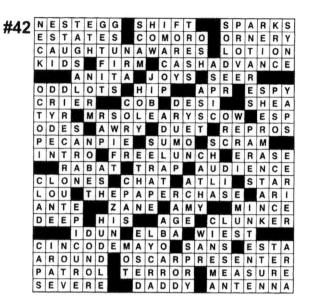

```
S C A B S   T S A R   L C D S   S K U A S
M O U R N   A U R A   A L I A   T N O T E
E Y D I E   V I K K I C A R R   R O M A N
L E I C A   E S S E N E S   I S E C O N D
T R E K K E R S   F U S S   P A K
      K E R N E L S   P O T L I K K E R S
U M P I R E   E T C   F R A T   N L A T
F A I L S   I D E A L S   A B E B E A M E
O X E N   A N A   B A I R D   L E T O N
S I D   O L A V S   R N A   D E A D E S T
      N E W Y O R K K N I C K S
C U P C A K E   L A K   A L C E E   C B S
A S A H I   M O N E T   W A D   J A P E
R E S U R V E Y   I N A T U B   A A R O N
O N E K   I V O R   T R A   E C C L E S
B O O K K E E P E R   O U T L O O K
      A W W   E T E S   H A N U K K A H
S E A B A S S   A N O F F E R   S N I D E
W A G O N   W K K E L L O G G   T I N E A
A R R O Z   A L E G   I R A E   I F E L L
P L A T A   M U S E   T A P S   C E R E S
```

#42

```
N E S T E G G   S H I F T   S P A R K S
E S T A T E S   C O M O R O   O R N E R Y
C A U G H T U N A W A R E S   L O T I O N
K I D S   F I R M   C A S H A D V A N C E
      A N I T A   J O Y S   S E E R
O D D L O T S   H I P   A P R   E S P Y
C R I E R   C O B   D E S I   S H E A
T Y R   M R S O L E A R Y S C O W   E S P
O D E S   A W R Y   D U E T   R E P R O S
P E C A N P I E   S U M O   S C R A M
I N T R O   F R E E L U N C H   E R A S E
      R A B A T   T R A P   A U D I E N C E
C L O N E S   C H A T   A T L I   S T A R
L O U   T H E P A P E R C H A S E   A R I
A N T E   Z A N E   A M Y   M I N C E
D E E P   H I S   A G E   C L U N K E R
      I D U N   E L B A   W I E S T
C I N C O D E M A Y O   S A N S   E S T A
A R O U N D   O S C A R P R E S E N T E R
P A T R O L   T E R R O R   M E A S U R E
S E V E R E   D A D D Y   A N T E N N A
```

#43

```
G A S P S   R A M P   F L E S H   B O S C
E C L A T   A M O R   L O N E R   O L I O
E L I T E   B I P O L A R D I S O R D E R
S U P E R M A N   S A G A S   R E E V E
      O R N O T   S P Y O N   B L A R N E Y
O F F S E T   C L E O N   T R O T
R O T O R   W H A R F   S O U W E S T E R
C A H N   S H I P O F S T A T E   T I L E
A L E   D I E T S   P O S E   L A P E L
      T H E R E S   S H O O T   S A L O M E
C H O I C E S   S L O O P   B E N E F I T
L O N D O N   T H O R N   F E W E S T
A N G E R   G R A M   T A L E S   H M O
S O U R   F L I P O N E S L I D   B E A D
P R E S C R I B E   A C A S E   A R I S E
      R U D E   S P O R E   C R I C K S
P O S T A G E   R O O T S   S T A G E
E T H A N   E A R L Y   C A N N I B A L
S H O R E S O F T R I P O L I   S T E R E
T E N T   A N G I O   E L A N   A T R I A
O R E S   N O H O W   S E N T   S E G A R
```

#44

```
W E N T A W A Y   S T E P P E   A B H O R
A L I E N A T E   H O L I E R   M O O G Y
C A N N Y C A N D A N C E R S   U L T R A
O N E D   N S A   T I C K E T   E D E N
      H O T E   R H O D E   Y O Y O S
M O O N Y J U I C E   S N A R I N G
E N L   P E N H   A H S   E T A L   B A A
I C E   E C T O   L E C T E R N   S U D S
R E S T S T O P   T R I E D I T   E N D S
      R E S   S H O   A L S   V E N U E
A S C O T   B O N Y D E R E K   E G Y P T
V I R U S   U P A   O W S   G R E
A T O P   I T E R A T E   C O L O R A D O
S A N E   T A N K F U L   O M A N   L E O
T R Y   Z A N E   C S A   M E D I   F E N
      M A I L E R S   M E A N Y C U L P A
P A T T I   K R E B S   S A G A
I A G O   C E R E A L   S S R   A N K A
M I N D Y   D O W N Y J O N E S I N D E X
A N O D E   T S E T S E   A N E C D O T E
M E N S A   V E R S E D   P E A S A N T S
```

#45

```
C O A T S   O B A M A   C A V A L C A D E
I N D I A   T R E E S   O V E R E A T E R
G E O R G E B U R N S   M A R K T W A I N
A G R E E D   S O L E S   S S E
R A N D   I T S   O T O O L E   M A R S H
      O N C E   D I O D E   C A T O
A B R A H A M L I N C O L N   L I T T E R
D O I N G   S T O R M Y   B E M U S E D
D O C T O R   E N O   A L C A P O N E
E N C O D E   S M A C K   R U T S
R E I N   C H A S M   E L M E R   R E D S
      G E O L   E L R O Y   I T A L I C
B O B F O S S E   U N D   C A B A N A
E V E R E S T   A L L E G E   W A T E R
G A L O R E   S H E L L E Y W I N T E R S
A T O M   S L O A N   E A S Y
N E W E L   I N S I S T   S N L   R A Y S
      A R N   N O R T H   A N I M A L
G O R E V I D A L   M U H A M M A D A L I
A M E R I C A N O   M E A D E   P E T I T
D I A G N O S I S   E R R E D   A R I E S
```

#46
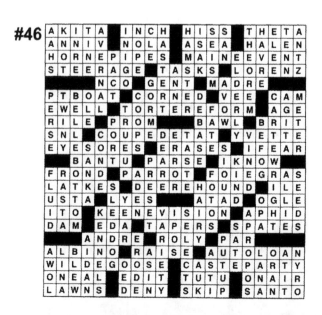

```
A K I T A   I N C H   H I S S   T H E T A
A N N I V   N O L A   A S E A   H A L E N
H O R N E P I P E S   M A I N E E V E N T
S T E E R A G E   T A S K S   L O R E N Z
      N C O   G E N T   M A D R E
P T B O A T   C O R N E D   V E E   C A M
E W E L L   T O R T E R E F O R M   A G E
R I L E   P R O M   B A W L   B R I T
S N L   C O U P E D E T A T   Y V E T T E
E Y E S O R E S   E R A S E S   I F E A R
      B A N T U   P A R S E   I K N O W
F R O N D   P A R R O T   F O I E G R A S
L A T K E S   D E E R E H O U N D   I L E
U S T A   L Y E S   A T A D   O G L E
I T O   K E E N E V I S I O N   A P H I D
D A M   E D A   T A P E R S   S P A T E S
      A N D R E   R O L Y   P A R
A L B I N O   R A I S E   A U T O L O A N
W I L D E G O O S E   C A S T E P A R T Y
O N E A L   E D I T   T U T U   O N A I R
L A W N S   D E N Y   S K I P   S A N T O
```

#47

```
TEEN  LEAP  SPLAT  ARTES
INDO  AWNS  ERICA  LIETO
ANGRYMENINAFILM  IFSAY
RUE  AERO  ELI  UPS  LSTS
AIRER  USHERS  ALBEE
  ADORNER  MAC  ISOLDE
FAIRWAYCLUB  BOATTRAIN
LON  ORNE  APOOR  APTTO
ARMORS  ITLL  LORRIES
STALK  LOLITA  AMESS
HAND  WINKSINANAP  TOSS
  OMINE  AMENTS  MOUTH
  ABLATES  NODE  COLTER
ALADY  ATHER  EGAD  DEE
CARSTEREO  EARLYRECORD
HITMAN  PEN  PALMYRA
  HOGAN  SOLIDI  ABATE
LOEB  SYD  REA  PRAT  FOR
ALLIS  TENMINUTESOFTWO
DIMLY  OCTAL  RINK  ARES
SNEER  LIANA  ICES  DARE
```

#48

```
DAS  BAP  ARTISTE  DOER
ESP  IFS  PERSIAN  LORNE
ATINGLE  PEELERS  SWATS
NINE⨯OUTOFTEN  AUNTIE
  SPADES  NOUS  TORT
SEPTET  PED  HALF⨯CORES
ACTIN  RESUME  DOGIE
GOANDSEE  LAMP  SONATAS
  GETS  GUNSEL  CRAMP
GAP  RICKETY  DOLT  TRUE
OBIT  LUNCH⨯TAPLE  HOSE
OATH  LEEK  ORLEANS  TED
SCARF  WOLVES  MOAN
EASEOFF  SEEP  MARMOSET
  ENRON  TRIBES  SWISH
BED⨯TORIES  DID  SHINTO
ANOA  STAN  GESTES
BULLET  DAY⨯OAPOPERAS
BRIAN  LAPBELT  ONAROLL
LENDL  AVIATOR  OER  AGE
EDGY  DENSITY  LSD  RAD
```

#49

```
RAIN  JBARS  PDAS  VERNE
ACNE  ALTAI  LIST  ADEER
TRAGEDIANS  APPELLANTS
SENATES  TACOS  ALMOST
  SETT  SCLERAL  ABES
  EAR  AERATE  ROY  DBA
  NURSE  POSSESSOR  SEAS
DENS  TOE  ISE  NESS
EST  REPRISAL  TERRAPIN
ATHEIST  TALONS  ERSE
  INSTS  ARISE  TEPEE
  ANTE  SLAVER  INADAZE
ANKERITE  SEROLOGY  TOW
HEIR  TON  ANI  DELE
SANS  ENTRAINED  NARDA
ORG  HRE  ARSENE  EVE
  WEAR  PRICERS  ASNO
ATTAIN  SPENT  CONSIST
REINSTATES  ACCEPTANCE
MANET  MORT  RHONE  GEAN
SLEDS  PASS  SATES  ERRS
```

CONTENTED, AT LAST!

#50

```
ONEA†  BEN†  CALI  UN†ED
TENET  CADI  OMAN  TOOTH
RICHARDSON  ROCKGUNNEL
OLEOLE  ELG  DOE  OBSESS
  PUKA  LAGOONS  BEES
WAHS  URN  CHIP
EDAMES  DRABBLE  SERENE
LALALA  OUR  LEN  ONEACT
STONED  UND  EAT  UNTRUE
HEN  ADOBES  UNHATS  TRY
  LAL  ROH
SUR  HERETO  †BONES  MTA
THEMOB  †UP  TAN  ROSARY
EUDORA  EME  ORE  NUTRIA
RR†ING  SINEWED  †PATCH
SAKS  SSN  TIES
  NTSB  SMEARED  SPIN
AMIENS  EOS  IVE  ERODED
MAGNACARTA  VETERINARY
ASHER  ATOM  ARES  MELBA
DETRE  LA†E  LYRE  PREEN
```

MAKE YOUR PUZZLE COLLECTION COMPLETE
with Simon & Schuster's Convenient Backlist Order Form

Now in its ninth decade of publication.

The Original Crossword Puzzle Series

0-684-81473-0	#195	Feb. 97	Samson	$9.00
0-684-86936-5	#218	Feb. 01	Samson	$9.00
0-684-86937-3	#219	Apr. 01	Samson	$9.95
0-684-86938-1	#220	Jun. 01	Samson	$9.95
0-684-86941-1	#222	Oct. 01	Samson	$9.95
0-7432-0537-5	#223	Dec. 01	Samson	$9.95
0-7432-5096-6	#236	Feb. 04	Samson	$9.95
0-7432-5111-3	#237	Apr. 04	Samson	$9.95
0-7432-5112-1	#238	Jun. 04	Samson	$9.95
0-7432-5121-0	#239	Aug. 04	Samson	$9.95
0-7432-5122-9	#240	Oct. 04	Samson	$9.95
0-7432-5123-7	#241	Dec. 04	Samson	$9.95
0-7432-5124-5	#242	Feb. 05	Samson	$9.95
0-7432-5125-3	#243	Apr. 05	Samson	$9.95
0-7432-5126-1	#244	Jun. 05	Samson	$9.95
0-7432-5127-X	#245	Aug. 05	Samson	$9.95
0-7432-5128-8	#246	Oct. 05	Samson	$9.95
0-7432-5129-6	#247	Dec. 05	Samson	$9.95
0-7432-8313-9	#248	Jan. 06	Samson	$9.95
0-7432-8314-7	#249	Apr. 06	Samson	$9.95
0-7432-8315-5	#250	Jun. 06	Samson	$9.95
0-7432-8316-3	#251	Aug. 06	Samson	$9.95
0-7432-8317-1	#252	Oct. 06	Samson	$9.95
0-7432-8318-X	#253	Dec. 06	Samson	$9.95

Simon & Schuster Crossword Treasuries

0-684-84366-8	#40	Sept. 99	Samson	$9.00
0-684-85637-9	S&S 75th Anniversary Vintage Crossword Treasury			
		Apr. 99	Farrar	$9.00
0-7432-4795-7	#41	Nov. 03	Samson/Maleska	$10.00
0-7432-7056-8	#42	Dec. 05	Samson	$10.00

Simon & Schuster Crostics

0-671-87193-5	#111	July 94	Middleton	$8.00
0-684-81380-7	#114	Nov. 95	Middleton	$8.00
0-684-82963-0	#116	Nov. 96	Middleton	$8.00
0-684-83652-1	#117	Aug. 97	Middleton	$8.00

Simon & Schuster Crostics Treasuries

0-671-87221-4	#3	Mar. 94	Middleton	$8.00
0-684-84354-4	#5	Mar. 98	Middleton	$9.00
0-7432-0059-4	#6	Nov. 00	Middleton	$9.00

Simon & Schuster Fun with Crostics Series

0-684-84277-7	#20	Jan. 98	Duerr	$8.00
0-684-84361-7	#21	Jun. 98	Duerr	$8.00
0-684-85942-4	#24	July 99	Duerr	$8.00

Simon & Schuster Super Crostics Books

0-671-51132-7	#3	Mar. 95	Middleton	$10.00
0-684-81340-8	#4	Mar. 97	Middleton	$10.00
0-684-84364-1	#5	Mar. 99	Middleton	$10.00

Simon & Schuster Super Crossword Books

0-671-79232-6	#7	Nov. 92	Maleska	$10.00
0-671-89709-8	#8	Nov. 94	Maleska	$10.00
0-684-82964-9	#9	Nov. 96	Maleska	$10.00
0-684-84365-X	#10	Oct. 98	Samson	$10.00
0-684-87186-6	#11	May 01	Samson	$10.00
0-7432-5538-0	#12	Nov. 04	Samson/Maleska	$10.00
0-7432-9321-5	#13	Nov. 06	Samson	$10.00

Simon & Schuster Large Type Crossword Puzzle Books

0-684-81187-1	#1	Oct. 95	Maleska	$10.00
0-684-84367-6	#3	Nov. 99	Maleska	$9.00

Savage Crossword Puzzle Series

0-684-87195-5	#1	Jul. 00	Savage	$12.00
0-684-87196-3	#2	Mar. 01	Savage	$12.00

S&S Super Crossword Puzzle Dictionary and Reference Book

0-684-85696-4		Apr. 99	$15.00

SEND ORDERS TO:

Simon & Schuster Inc.
Order Processing
Department

100 Front Street
Riverside, NJ 08075
Customer Service:
1-800-223-2336
Fax: 1-800-943-9831

Total Cost of All Books Ordered _____

Add Applicable State Sales Tax _____

Check or Money Order Enclosed for _____

Please Charge VISA _____ MASTERCARD _____ AMEX _____

Card # _____ Exp. Date _____

Signature _____

Ship to:

Name _____

Address _____

City _____ State _____ Zip Code _____

PLEASE NOTE:
Prices subject to change without prior notice. If any part of your order is out of stock when we receive it, we will ship available titles and will send a refund for the portion we cannot fill.

FIRESIDE
A Division of Simon & Schuster
A VIACOM COMPANY